HAUNTED
VIRGINIA CITY

JANICE OBERDING

Haunted
America

Published by Haunted America
A Division of The History Press
Charleston, SC 29403
www.historypress.net

CONTENTS

CONTENTS

CONTENTS

FOREWORD

So, you want a good ghost story? Well, you have come to the right place. Virginia City was named one of the top-three most haunted towns in America. On any given day or night, you will find people who come to Virginia City in the hope of having a ghostly encounter, or they want to share their experience with someone who won't think they are crazy. You can walk down the boardwalk on a quiet night and hear footsteps behind you, only to turn and find no one there. Did you feel a cold, ghostly hand on your shoulder? Don't worry—it happens all the time. Almost every building here has its ghost and its stories and tales of those who lived here long ago. Virginia City is not alone in being a living ghost town—Nevada is full of them—but there is a difference here on "the Hill." You can feel it the moment your feet hit the boardwalk: a feeling that will make you want to come back over and over.

Virginia City is home to an eclectic gathering of not only people but also history and legends, all so colorful and unique. The people I have met in this small hillside town have all taken up a spot in my heart, making a beautiful quilt.

There is specialness to this town, and the conversations you have with the people here are like none you can have anywhere else. If you ask where a certain someone is, the unexpected reply might be, "Oh, she is off racing camels in Hawaii." There is one particular gentleman who had the best stories about his time on the sharpshooter circuit, and he was also involved in the very last shootout on the streets of Virginia City (many, many years ago). The people come and go, but I think those who have spent time here on the Comstock leave a tiny part of their soul when they go, adding to the color and richness of this town. Perhaps that is why it is so haunted.

I first met Janice some six years ago when my friend Tom and I decided to start giving ghost tours. I had bought one of her books, and after reading it, I knew that if I was going to do ghost tours, I needed to meet her. Among her friends and many fans, she is referred to as the "First Lady of Haunted Nevada," and she is truly among the pioneers of the paranormal field. Janice and I share a great love for this town, both its history and ghost stories.

Over the years, the experiences I have had in Virginia City run the gamut of the paranormal. I have seen full-bodied apparitions and seen objects move, and I have had whispers in my ear—the list goes on and on. I have interacted with Rosie, the prostitute at the Silver Queen Hotel. She is very nice, especially if we have men on the tour. Tom has had quite a few encounters with the Shadow Man at the Washoe Club, but be careful—he does like to throw things.

Now, read this book, and then come to Virginia City to have your own ghostly encounter. We're waiting for you.

—Debbie Bender
Virginia City historian and the owner/operator of
Bats in the Belfry Virginia City Ghost Tours

ACKNOWLEDGEMENTS

Writing is lonely work. The writer works alone, and yet no book would come to fruition without the help of others. There are many people I wish to acknowledge and thank for their help in this book (and other books as well). First, I must thank my lovely mother, Bonnie Harper, who took an old typewriter and a ream of paper and forged a writing path for me to follow. Mama's love of books and writing is part of my earliest and most cherished memories, and her encouragement and guidance have seen me through some challenging days and nights of writing. Thank you to my one-in-a-million husband, Bill, who is always there for me, who understands even when I'm antisocial, oblivious and writing; his suggestions and photography are invaluable. Thanks to my beautiful sister Diane Grulke, a writer herself, whose help with research, writing conversations and suggestions are deeply appreciated. Thank you to my dear friend Terri Hall-Peltier, whose friendship I treasure as much as I do her willingness to photograph, share her experiences and explore. Thanks are also due to my dear friend Deborah Carr-Senger for her encouragement, the road trips, writing suggestions and her wit and charm. Thank you to my longtime friend the multitalented Kristin Hamlet, a remarkable researcher historian and Virginia City expert, who always has time to get at the truth. Thanks to my adventuresome friend Debbie Bender, owner of Bats in the Belfry Virginia City Ghost Tours, for sharing her stories, experiences and knowledge of Virginia City. Thank you to my friends of many years, Sharon Leong and Anne Leong, whose beautiful photography has added so much to my work over the years. Thank you to

ACKNOWLEDGEMENTS

Paula Burris for her wisdom and sense of humor, stories and experiences with a weird clock; Angela Colman, for being a great friend who willingly shared her knowledge and experiences of Virginia City, especially St. Mary's Art Center; special thank you to my friend Richard St. Clair of Empathic Paranormal for sharing his time, and his experiences with the paranormal; Reno Apparition Seekers Society (RASS) members Jeff Frey, Jason Ball and Bruce Pollard for sharing ghost experiences and photographs; and Wayne Pierce for sharing his knowledge and experiences ghost investigating in Virginia City. Special thanks to my dear, sweet friend Virginia Ridgway, whose ideas and wisdom have guided me in the right direction—most of the time. Thanks to my daughter-in-law Peggy, who accompanied me on many early Virginia City ghost hunts, and to the many ghost investigators who have shared my enthusiasm for hunting ghosts in Virginia City over the years. Finally, since no book would get published without a publisher's go ahead, I want to thank Artie Crisp and the people at The History Press for saying yes to my ideas and for bringing them to viable book form.

INTRODUCTION

It's been said that every place is haunted. This is probably true, especially in Virginia City. Is there a town with more ghosts? I doubt it. Virginia City has the title of being the third-most haunted city in the United States. I disagree. In fact, I would argue that it is the *most* haunted city in the United States. That's my opinion; I say it without reservation, and I'm not going to change it anytime soon.

The ghost enthusiasts who trek up Geiger Grade to Virginia City regularly will most likely agree with me on this. Along with the ghost enthusiasts come the TV stars and history buffs. There's a reason for this.

But my bias is showing. You see, Virginia City has always been a special place to me. The first time I saw the town, I was a child. It was midsummer. The heat was intense, and we were here to see where the Cartwrights of television's *Bonanza* fame roamed. As my stepdad skillfully eased the family station wagon around each curve, he explained that the road was so steep and narrow that drivers had to honk their horns as warning to oncoming cars. Looking out the window I could clearly see that, yes, it was a long way down. Cartwrights or not, was this trek up the hill really worth all this, I wondered. Once in Virginia City (VC to the locals), I had my answer. There is no place on earth quite like Virginia City. Many years have come and gone since that long-ago summer day. My opinion of this tiny town on Mount Davidson remains the same.

My husband and I got our marriage license at the Storey County Courthouse in Virginia City. As we drove south on Virginia Street, we glanced over and happened to notice that a Harrahs limousine was beside us in the next lane; a celebrity was onboard. But who? The star was Joey Bishop.

"Hey, Joey," we called out to him.

To our delight, he acknowledged us with a wave and a smile. Then, like strangers in the night, we went our separate ways. The limo turned right at 341 toward Lake Tahoe, and we turned left toward VC.

Just about every building on the Comstock has a ghostly resident or haunting tale. And that's the fun of Virginia City. You never know who, or what, you'll run into as you explore the town's historic treasures. Will you encounter a ghost? There are no guarantees. But then, with more residents in the cemetery than on the census rolls you never can tell.

Take a stroll down the boardwalk and you'll be retracing the footsteps of ghost hunters like Zak Bagans, Nick Groff, Aaron Goodwin, Jason Hawes and Grant Wilson. Long before the aforementioned came to Virginia City in search of ghosts, Mark Twain was taking great joy in poking fun of people who spoke to the dead, while Comstock journalist Alf Doten was using the dial (precursor to the Ouija board) to do just that. Eilley Bowers was conversing with the dead using a peep stone (crystal ball), and early spiritualists were holding regular séances for the same purpose. Interest in ghosts is nothing new. Perhaps some of these early séances are responsible for the number of ghosts and hauntings in Virginia City. Surely they are responsible for the special aura the Comstock possesses to this very day.

Like other ghost hunting historians, I think history is crucial to the investigation of the paranormal. So, too, are lore and legend. Like history, these tell us about the people who live in a specific location, and by knowing more about a locale's people, we also gain a better understanding of its ghosts. It can often be an arduous task for the historian to separate fact from fiction. There is primary source material, and some of it is very good. But what if you have two primary source materials from two different viewpoints on a particular incident? When examining primary source material, we should keep in mind that these primary sources are told/written from individual perspectives, and the biases of the time period should be obvious. Primary sources can and occasionally do slant the facts. Therefore I find myself unable to trust completely some primary source materials, unless they are sound recordings, newsreels and motion pictures of a specific time period and incident. The fact that such methods didn't exist in the mid-nineteenth century demonstrates the problem.

INTRODUCTION

This book presents history—and how could a book about ghosts not? Certainly, ghosts are of the past, and we all know there is no changing the past. But history is different. It is not a relic that exists only in the withering pages of faded old diaries, yellowing love letters written by long-dead lovers, newspapers or any other primary source materials. History is mutable. We will always discover different things about the past. The history that we hold as sacrosanct could change with a new discovery tomorrow.

Lore, legend and firsthand experiences are presented within these pages as well. First and foremost, this is a book about Virginia City's ghosts. To those who would deny the existence of ghosts, I will say that, yes, it is true that we have no defining evidence or proof that ghosts and hauntings exist. But aren't they fun (most of them, anyway) to experience?

It is my hope that this book will make you, the reader, want to get in your car and drive to Virginia City (from wherever you may live), for this is a little town not to be overlooked by those seeking to enjoy themselves, discover Nevada's early day mining history and hunt ghosts.

Come on up the hill and see what this town is all about. As author Dolores K. O'Brien said in her wonderful little 1968 book *Meet Virginia City's Ghosts*, "Our ghosts have been waiting for you."

Indeed they are.

CHAPTER 1

RUSH TO WASHOE

QUEST FOR SILVER

THE UNFORTUNATE GROSH BROTHERS

If anyone has a reason to haunt the canyon areas around Virginia City, it would be Hosea and Ethan Allen Grosh. And yet, their ghosts don't seem to wander here. Their tragic story starts with the California gold rush that began in 1848 with James Marshall's gold discovery on the American River in California. Thousands of men said goodbye to families and friends and headed west. In the spring of 1849, the two sons of Reverend Aaron B. Grosh said farewell to friends and family in Reading, Pennsylvania, and set out for the placer mines of California.

Like so many others, they arrived at the placer mines of El Dorado County in search of spectacular riches. Urged on by dreams of gold nuggets sparkling in the streams and rivers of California, they stayed long after the gold rush ended. Still clinging to their hopes of striking it rich, they waited for the next big opportunity. Before that chance came, California became a state. On that same day in 1850, the United States Congress, by Organic Act, created the Utah Territory, which incorporated most of what is modern-day Nevada.

In 1852, word began to spread of a gold discovery in the far-flung region of the Utah Territory. Like they had to California, men came scurrying to Gold Canyon (near present-day Virginia City) in search of the riches that had eluded them in California. Among them were Hosea and Ethan Allen Grosh. They soon learned that this region of the Utah Territory was vastly

Welcome to Virginia City. *Photo by Bill Oberding.*

The view of Virginia City from Silver Terrace Cemetery. *Photo by Bill Oberding.*

different from lush and green California. This was a land of sagebrush, scraggly pines, dust and rock. Unlike the gold rush of California, where gold was found in rivers and streams, this gold was located in an arid, high desert region, and it was being pulled from the ground. There wasn't much, but it was enough to assuage gold fever. Only the strong would preserve in this influx that would be known as the Rush to Washoe.

Of all the men (and women) who came seeking silver in the Utah Territory, Hosea Ballou and Ethan Allen Grosh would suffer such bad luck that they almost seemed cursed. The original discoverers of the Comstock Lode, the Grosh brothers should have ended up being the wealthiest men in the territory. Instead, they were the most tragic. While the two brothers worked beside other prospectors, they noticed men tossing a rich blue-colored ore aside as worthless, and their interest was piqued. Better educated than most of the men here in the canyon, they thought of silver—silver that could make them very rich. They wisely told no one of their suspicions. Let the other men meet and socialize late into the evening. Not the Grosh brothers, who returned to their Johnstown cabin each night to pore over their many metallurgical books. The more they read and analyzed the ore samples, the more convinced they became that the blue stuff scorned by the other miners was indeed silver. Sharing their find with their father, they wrote in November 3, 1856: "We found two veins of silver at the forks of Gold Canyon…one of these veins is a perfect monster."

Nineteen days later, on November 22, 1856, they wrote, "We have hopes almost amounting to certainty of veins crossing the canyon at two other points."

To be certain it was silver, they would need to analyze the ore further. But this would take more money than either of them had. So they headed back to El Dorado County, California, for the winter. Hoping to make enough to finance their operations in the Utah Territory, they prospected for quartz.

When they returned to Gold Canyon in the spring, they were still short of cash and still as determined to locate and claim the rich veins they suspected were in the canyon.

On June 8, 1857, Ethan Allen wrote to their father.

> We struck the vein in Gold Cañón. A dark gray mass, tarnished probably, by the sulfuric acid in the water. It resembles thin sheet lead, broken very fine—and lead the miners suppose it to be. The ore we found at the forks of the canyon; a large quartz vein at least, boulders from a vein close by here shows itself. Other ore of silver we think we have found in the canyon, and a rock called black rock—very abundant—we think contains silver.

They located what they referred to as our monster vein—the silver veins that crossed Mount Davidson—and quickly staked their claim. Then they set out to assay the ores. With an assay value of approximately $3,500 per ton, the silver would indeed make very rich men of them. When Ethan Allen wrote to his father, "We have had very bad luck," he couldn't have known that he and his brother would be besieged by that bad luck until the end of their short lives.

While working one sweltering August morning, Hosea missed his mark and struck his foot with the pickaxe. He soaked the deep wound in water and carefully bandaged it. Unfortunately, this wasn't enough to stop the terrible infection. Blood poisoning set in, and Hosea died two weeks later on September 2, 1858.

Ethan Allen was inconsolable. On September 7, 1858, he wrote to his father, informing him of Hosea's death:

> *In the first burst of my sorrow I complained bitterly of the dispensation which deprived me of what I held most dear of all the world, and I thought it most hard that he should be called away just as we had fair hopes of realizing what we had labored for so hard for so many years. But when I reflected how well an upright life had prepared him for the next, and what a debt of gratitude I owed to God in blessing me for so many years with so a dear companion, I became calm and bowed my head in resignation. "O Father thy will, not mine, be done." Our happy faith in the perfection of God's wisdom and goodness will be your consolation as this cloud passes over your head, for well I know your heart is full of the great hope which caused Paul to shout in triumph, "O death where is thy sting! O grave where is thy victory!"*

On September 11, 1858, Ethan Allen again wrote to his father:

> *I feel very lonely and miss Hosea very much—so much that at times I am strongly tempted to abandon everything and leave the country forever, cowardly as such a course would be. But I shall go on; it is my duty, and I cannot bear to give anything up until I bring it to a conclusion. By Hosea's death you fall heir to his share in the enterprise. We have, so far four veins. Three of them promise much.*

Ethan Allen Grosh was not a quitter. After paying his creditors and leaving Henry Comstock to safeguard his personal possessions and his cabin, Ethan

Allan packed up his ore samples and started for California with his friend R.M. Bucke in late October.

Like that of the ill-fated Donner Party, the arduous journey should never have been attempted this late in the year. The men encountered one mishap after another. Halfway toward their destination, they found themselves trapped by heavy snowstorms that were raging in the Sierras. When their food supply dwindled, they were forced to slaughter their mule. Finally, their matches became soaked, and they could no longer stay warm by a fire.

Later, Bucke would say that if not for Grosh's refusal to give up, he would have stopped there and died. Spurred on by Ethan Allen Grosh's determination, they walked in knee-deep snow for four days before being rescued. Their legs were badly frostbitten, and desperate measures were needed. One of Bucke's legs was amputated. But Ethan Allan refused a similar surgery. The decision cost him his life. He died on December 19, 1858, three months after his beloved brother Hosea's death.

The Ghost of Henry Comstock

What became of the Grosch brothers' silver? Henry Comstock was a man who knew opportunity when it knocked at his door. When he received word of Ethan Allen's death, he quickly helped himself to the brothers' maps and other mining implements. He claimed, as his own, that area in the canyon where the Grosch brothers had discovered their monster vein. Within the year, Patrick McLaughlin and Peter O'Riley made a discovery in Six-Mile Canyon to which Henry Comstock and his partner, Emanuel Penrod, laid claim. McLaughlin and O'Riley agreed to cut Comstock and his partner in. This was the rich Ophir Mine that would bring people from all over the world in search of silver and untold wealth during the Rush to Washoe.

Henry Comstock consulted those in the spirit realm regularly, paying strict attention to what they had to tell him. While most historians view Comstock as a lazy opportunist, he managed to get the richest silver lode in the history of the world named after him. But like the luckless Grosh brothers, Comstock would be dealt a bad hand by fate. He hastily sold his share of the mining claim for $10,000, very little considering the millions that it would one day be worth. Easy come, easy go, and before he knew it, Henry Comstock was broke again. He left Nevada sick and friendless. In

1870, he was living in Montana when, one day for no apparent reason, he picked up his pistol and shot himself to death.

He is buried at the Sunset Hills Cemetery in Bozeman, Montana. However, he prefers to haunt Virginia City. Four years after his death, strange lights were seen in the Ophir Mine. Worse, the sounds of someone far below using a pickaxe emanated up from the depths. No one wanted to go down and investigate. Finally, a young Irishman agreed to find out what was going on. With his friends teasing him about what he might find, he bravely stepped into the cage. And as it slowly lowered to the seven-hundred-foot level, he hoped he wouldn't find anything unearthly. The cage jerked to a stop, and he got out. There it was again, the sound of a pickaxe chipping away. He waved his lantern in the direction of the sound and gasped. The rotting corpse–like ghost of Henry Comstock leered at him. "I'm Henry Comstock, and this is mine!" the ghost screamed.

"I know, I know," the young man agreed. "I came down to see what was causing all the ruckus, and now I'll just go back up." He stepped back into the cage, giving the signal for it to be raised.

The ghostly Comstock laughed wickedly, "Don't ever come back!"

This isn't the last time the ghost of Henry Comstock has been spotted. He watches over his Ophir Mine site above ground, too. More than once, his haggard ghost has been seen angrily standing guard near his mine.

OLD VIRGINNY

Separating fact from fiction is not always an easy endeavor for the historian. This is especially true in regard to James Finney, aka Old Virginny. Did he really get drunk one night, break his bottle of whiskey in the street and proclaim the town to be Virginia (City)? According to legend, he did just that, and perhaps he did. After all, he was said to be from Virginia. This may have happened in a moment of homesickness. So there it is—legend or not, James Old Virginny Finney is generally credited with naming Virginia City.

Old Virginny was no exception to the bad luck that seemed to have dogged early discoverers of the Comstock Lode. Considering that Finney was approximately forty-four years old when he died after his horse threw him, you have to wonder about that appellation "Old." Legends and stories abound. They say Old Virginny sleeps eternally at the Dayton Cemetery.

Sandy and Eilley Bowers: The First Comstock Millionaires

Their love story is the stuff of northern Nevada legends. In the nineteenth century, when a woman got married, she generally stayed married. Even when her husband turned out to be less than a knight in shining armor, she had no choice but to look the other way. There were little or no opportunities to do anything but stay in their marriages and raise their families, so women usually did just that. But not Eilley Orrum.

Other women might sulk in silence, but Eilley had no qualms about severing the bonds of matrimony when there was no other choice. When her second husband heeded the call of Brigham Young to return to Salt Lake, Eilley refused to go. Knowing full well this would mean divorce, she waved him on his way. Eilley loved Nevada, and by consulting her peep stone (crystal ball), she knew that another husband would eventually come along. He came in the form of Lemuel "Sandy" Bowers, a tall, handsome miner who stayed at Eilley's makeshift boardinghouse in Gold Canyon. To read more about Eilley and Sandy Bowers, see one of my other books, *Haunted Reno*.

Did I say the stuff of legends? I meant every word of it. When Sandy couldn't pay his rent, Eilley agreed to take a small portion of his mining claim in lieu of the rent. Theirs was a love match that really blossomed when they struck it rich in Gold Canyon. Shortly, Sandy and Eilley would become the first Comstock's millionaires; unfortunately, neither their luck nor their money held out. However, before it all went, Sandy and Eilley moved out of their Gold Canyon shanty and hired builders to construct the finest home in the state. The site they chose was not in Virginia City but just down Geiger Grade in Washoe Valley. In order to furnish the home as befitting to their elevated status in the community, the nouveau riche Bowerses prepared for a European trip. Once in Europe, they would purchase the finest carpets, fabrics and antiques. Yesterday, Eilley might have ladled up some miner's bowl of beans, but today she was Queen of the Comstock.

Before they embarked, the ever-generous Sandy wanted to share his good fortune with friends, so they hired out the fabulous International Hotel at the corner of Union and C Streets and threw themselves a bon voyage party. Everyone on the Comstock was invited. No expense was spared, and nothing was too good for the Bowerses' guests. All types of food and drink were offered. This was to be a party the Comstock would not soon forget. Champagne glasses were not allowed to remain empty. As costly delicacies from faraway San Francisco were served to his guests, Sandy proudly rose to speak: "I've had powerful good luck…so go ahead enjoy yourselves. I've got money to throw at the birds."

It wasn't boastfulness, but a simple statement of fact. Sandy Bowers's wealth and good-hearted generosity were legendary among his fellow miners. While in Europe, Eilley attempted to visit Queen Victoria. She'd even had an elegant lavender dress created for the occasion. Victoria was not impressed with upstart miners' wives or twice-divorced women, and so the queen declined to meet with Eilley. A long-told tale is that of Eilley and the ivy. So offended by Victoria's snub, she went home to Bowers Mansion and pulled up all the ivy plants said to have been taken from cuttings of Buckingham Palace.

When he died a few years later, the vultures had all but picked Sandy's financial bones clean. Left penniless, Eilley started giving readings and telling fortunes to survive. But that's another story. Today, the Bowers Mansion still stands (unusual for Nevada) down in Washoe Valley, and back in Virginia City, the site of the International Hotel is the parking lot next to Grandma's Fudge. Several suicides and murders took place in the hotel. That might account for some of the weird activity that's been experienced here during the early morning hours. Maybe Sandy and Eilley's grand party continues on the other side. When all is silent, the saloons are closed, no one is on the streets and you can't even hear a hungry coyote howling in the distance, there is that faint sound of laughter and tinkling champagne glasses.

THE INTERNATIONAL HOTEL

The International Hotel was built at a cost of $14,000 and touted as the Hotel of the Territory. The brick building was three stories tall, featured a three-foot-high firewall on its roof and was far superior to the previous International Hotel that had occupied the same spot on the corner of Union and C Streets. An early advertisement proudly proclaimed, "The building is entirely fire-proof."

Unfortunately, this wasn't true. On the morning of October 26, 1875, a disastrous fire raged through Virginia City, leaving thousands of people homeless. More than one thousand buildings were destroyed. Among them was the fireproof International Hotel. Two years later, a third International Hotel was built at the same location. Far grander than those previous, the new hotel extended the entire block from C to B Streets, was six stories tall and had one hundred rooms and an elevator.

International Hotel. *Library of Congress.*

The International was the tallest building on the Comstock and the finest the area had ever known. San Francisco–bound stages left regularly from the hotel, and rooms went for as much as $500 per month. Many notables of the day stayed there, including Comstock millionaire John Mackay, who kept a permanent room at the hotel. When President Rutherford B. Hayes came to Virginia City on September 7, 1880, there was no question that he and his party would stay anywhere but at the International Hotel. From its C Street balcony, he gave a rousing speech to hundreds of cheering spectators.

Thirty-four years later, Virginia City lost its showpiece on a cold December morning in 1914, when a fire raged through the hotel, destroying it in a matter of hours. It's said that all hotels have their secrets, and the International is no exception. In his book *Elegance on C Street: The Story of the International Hotel*, author Richard Datin wrote of the Mystery Room. This particular room on the B Street side of the building was the site of numerous suicides. Several deaths took place in this room and at other spots in the hotel. It's certainly mysterious that the room most often involved in the deaths at the International was the only room out of 160 that hadn't burned. In fact, nothing within the room was destroyed in the fire.

Today the spot where the International once stood is a parking lot. Ghost hunters have recorded EVP and experienced other ghostly phenomena here in the wee hours of the morning. Could this be the ghostly Jimmy Cummings, who checked into the International Hotel on a cold, windy night in March 1900? Once inside his room, Cummings took a large dose of morphine and bid this world farewell. Things were closing in on Cummings, a mail clerk on the V&T passenger train. It was only a matter of time before he was arrested

The parking lot where the International Hotel once stood. *Photo by Bill Oberding.*

A crowd gathers at the site of the International Hotel celebrating the movie *Virginia City*, circa 1940s. Note the Silver Dollar Hotel and St. Mary's Art Center in the distance. *Author's collection.*

for robbing the mail. If convicted of the crime, Cummings knew he would be sentenced to more years in prison than he cared to think about. So he chose the easy way out. But was it?

Another who ended it all at the hotel was a man by the name of Si Brown, who went out onto the roof on October 23, 1871, and shot himself in the mouth. The reason for his fateful decision was said to have been an argument with his wife. Either of these men, or both, could still be haunting the parking lot.

There's also a good chance that Bill Smith haunts the spot. Smith died in the International Hotel saloon when Arthur Hefferner's pistol went off. Perhaps the unfortunate man isn't aware that he is dead or that so much time has passed since his death. Either way, I think that some of the ghosts at the old International Hotel location are responsible for paranormal activity at nearby Pipers Opera House and the Storey County Courthouse, as well as the Silver State National Peace Officers Museum.

Samuel Clemens Comes to Town

No question about it: Samuel Clemens was born in Hannibal, Missouri. Ah, but Mark Twain was born in Virginia City, Nevada. President Abraham Lincoln owed a favor, so he appointed attorney Orion Clemens as the territorial secretary of state for Nevada. Since his wife and daughter were unable to make the journey, Orion asked his younger brother Samuel to accompany him west. This promised to be a new adventure, and Samuel readily agreed.

Once in Nevada, Orion Clemens involved himself in state politics in Carson City while Samuel took a job at the *Territorial Enterprise* newspaper in Virginia City. There he met fellow writer William Wright, otherwise known as Dan De Quille. Both men enjoyed pointing out the failings and foibles of their fellow humans, and a friendship that would last the rest of their lives was quickly formed.

Twain had finally found his niche. He settled in and began writing editorials and the tall tales that would one day lead him to write *Roughing It*, which tells of his life in Virginia City. Twain's stay in Virginia City was a short one in his literary career, and he returned only a few times. He lectured at Pipers Opera House and wrote a correspondence for the larger newspapers. There are some who believe his lonely spirit still walks the streets of Virginia City late at night. If we accept the belief that ghosts can appear any way they choose—that is, an old person can appear as he or she did in youth—then we can understand why Mark Twain's ghost might be that of his young and robust self. We should also remember that Twain never knew Virginia City as an elderly man. Consider the following story that was told to me several years ago.

Since he lived only a short distance from C Street, a man who liked to drink in one of the local saloons seldom drove, except in snowy or rainy weather. On this particular night, he'd stayed longer than usual and wanted nothing more than the warmth of his bed. He said goodbye to the barkeep and started walking toward home. As he sauntered down the boardwalk, he encountered a young man who appeared to be dressed as Mark Twain.

"Nice getup. Where ya goin'?" he asked the stranger, thinking there was a party somewhere in town that he hadn't heard about. Without a word, the stranger glared at him and dissolved into thin air. Even though he was positive that he'd met the ghost of Mark Twain, the man decided that this would be the last time he ever stayed so late at the saloon.

THE 601 VIGILANCE COMMITTEE

Maintaining law and order wasn't always easy in the early west. Vigilantes took law into their own hands when it seemed that a lawbreaker wouldn't be dealt with swiftly enough. Throughout Nevada and California, the vigilance committee was a secret society of men, formed to ensure the peace and safety of their towns. On the Comstock, the vigilance committee was known as the 601, and the committee meant business. When a man was told to leave town or suffer the consequences, he left town if he were a smart man. If not—well, the 601 wasn't opposed to lynching a law-breaking hombre who overstayed his welcome in its fair city.

Arthur Perkins Hefferner and George Kirk ignored the 601 and paid for their foolishness with their lives. Hefferner was enjoying a night on the town when he stopped in at the International Hotel's saloon. Full of liquor and bravado, he joked and insulted fellow bar patrons. Bill Smith was also full of liquor and bravado, and he teased back. Hefferner angrily pulled his revolver and asked Smith where he preferred to be shot. Before the poor man could respond, Hefferner's gun went off, shooting Smith in the face. Fatally wounded, he stumbled a few feet and dropped to the floor, dead. Hefferner was immediately taken to jail. This wasn't enough for the 601. A senseless murder had taken place, and the culprit would have to pay. Early in the pre-dawn morning, while most of the town slept or worked underground in the mines, the 601 broke into jail and escorted Hefferner to his doom. By all reports, Arthur Perkins Hefferner was calm as the group stealthily led him up A Street to Sutton and on up to the Ophir Mine. There, without benefit of a fair trial, judge or jury, the vigilantes quickly lynched him. His lifeless

A 601 sign on the E. Clampus Vitus Building in Virginia City. *Photo by Bill Oberding.*

body was discovered hours later. A note was pinned to his coat that read, "Arthur Perkins—Committee No. 601."

Everyone knew what that meant, and the lynching outraged many in Virginia City. But the 601 wasn't finished with taking the law into its own hands. When George Kirk was ordered to leave, he bravely decided to test the 601's resolve. He galloped off into the night, pretending to leave Virginia City forever. But when he thought it was safe, Kirk sneaked back into town and continued his drunken, disorderly behavior. No one could fool the 601 for long, however. When members of the group caught up with him, Kirk was taken to a gravel pit and summarily dispatched to the next world. But his widow lived several miles away in Ophir Canyon, so members of the 601 did the decent thing; they packed George Kirk's body on ice for three days until she was able to come to Virginia City and attend his funeral.

That these two deaths were injustice, there's no question. The question is who is the ghost that roams an area around the Storey County courthouse? Is it George Kirk or Arthur Perkins Hefferner? From the day of his death, rumors have persisted that the ghost of Arthur Perkins Hefferner still lingers. Perhaps he's seeking the justice he didn't receive in life. Then again, the specter could be that of George Kirk, promising to leave town forever if given a second chance.

CHAPTER 2
LORE, LEGEND AND HAUNTINGS

SILVER TERRACE CEMETERY

While some who came to Virginia City became wealthy beyond their wildest dreams, others were not so fortunate. Life was hard on the Comstock. Death came daily, making no distinctions. A man with a big bank account could succumb to disease or disaster just as easily as a man who barely had the price of a decent meal. In the end, those who died here were all headed for a plot at the Silver Terrace. The wealthy and the destitute all rested in peace beside one another—all except for the soiled doves, the women who worked in the brothels or on the streets. They were the outcasts and hence not fit to be buried beside others. This was commonplace in mid- to late nineteenth-century western towns.

While you enjoy the solitude and serenity that is Silver Terrace Cemetery, be aware that it sprawls on and on. It actually encompasses thirteen cemeteries, and burials still take place here. If the cemetery looks familiar, perhaps it is because it has been featured on numerous TV shows, including *Ghost Adventures* and *Antiques Roadshow*.

It's interesting to note just how few of Virginia City's most famous men and women are actually buried here. People like Eilley Bowers, Mark Twain, John and Louise Mackay and Julia Bulette are not buried at the Silver Terrace. This, of course, doesn't stop any of them from actively haunting their favorite Virginia City spots.

Silver Terrace Cemetery. *Photo by Bill Oberding.*

Another view of Silver Terrace Cemetery. *Photo by Bill Oberding.*

Silver Terrace Cemetery. *Photo by Bill Oberding.*

Because of problems in the past, there are laws against vandalizing the cemetery, and Virginia City legend clearly warns against it. But this hasn't stopped vandals from callously destroying much of the older headstones and ironwork. Perhaps these people don't mind the Storey County Jail or paying hefty fines. But being haunted and harassed by the occupant of a grave whose headstone they've toppled sure sounds like a miserable experience to me.

At the entrance gate is the grave site of one Mary Jane Simpson. Mary Jane was not a wife, a teacher or a courtesan. She was a mule that perished in the great fire of 1875. You may wonder about Mary Jane as you enter the Silver Terrace. You might even ask yourself why a mule is buried at the entrance to the cemetery. That's a good question. Permit me to ask another: why not?

Of special interest here is the mystery of the glowing headstone. Which headstone is it? The glowing headstone has been seen numerous times over the years, and yet no one is absolutely sure where it is. Locals claim to know precisely where it is, but they aren't telling. Others insist that there is nothing paranormal at all about the glowing headstone. The stone, they say, is made of a material that makes it appear to glow on certain nights. Some argue that the phenomenon is not a headstone at all but a ghostly young girl who rises from her grave on certain nights.

To explore the Silver Terrace, you'll need several hours and a comfortable pair of shoes. Step lightly and listen for rattlesnakes. One thing you'll notice

Trees are rare in the Silver Terrace Cemetery, but here one grew on a grave. *Photo by Bill Oberding*

Above: A group of graves.
Photo by Bill Oberding.

Right: An old grave and
tree. *Photo by Bill Oberding.*

is that here in the desert, our cemeteries are different from those in other regions. Don't expect any moss-draped trees, expanses of lush green lawns or memorial rose gardens here at the Silver Terrace. The cemetery is closed and locked at nightfall. If you want to explore during evening hours, you must get permission to do so. Good luck with that. It is almost impossible to be granted entrance after dark. Remember those vandals? So does the Storey County Sheriff Department. Violators who trespass are practically guaranteed to spend some time at the Storey County Jail.

THE MURDER OF JULIA BULETTE

If you happen to walk by the area of Union and D Streets late at night and happen to notice the shadowy figure of a woman staring forlornly after you, don't be alarmed. You may have encountered the ghost of Julia Bulette. This is the location of the little house where she lived and was brutally murdered.

Julia Bulette is well known in Virginia City; over the years, her name has been used for shops and restaurants. If not for Lucius Beebe and Charles Clegg, she might have rested in relative obscurity out near Flowery Hill. Julia was just another woman who lived and worked in the red-light district on D Street. Certainly, she wasn't the fabulously wealthy and oh-so-glamorous lady of the evening that she's often been portrayed as. Yet Julia was a favorite among the town's male population. When she had the bad luck of being murdered in her bed during the early morning hours of January 20, 1867, her place in Virginia City lore and legend was guaranteed. The murder outraged the men of the Comstock, who wanted the killer found and brought to justice as quickly as possible.

On the morning after her murder, the *Territorial Enterprise* carried a headline that read, "Horrible Murder—Woman Strangled in Her Bed—Blood-Curdling Tragedy Directly in the Heart of the City."

The location of her final resting place is not the only mystery surrounding the misfortunate Julia. While most historians agree that Julia Bulette posed for the photograph with fire hat no. 1, others believe the woman in the photo was actually the wife of a Virginia City fireman. Julia Bulette, they insist, was actually the beautiful Creole woman whose face graces a painting behind the bar of the Bucket of Blood Saloon. In their 1950 book *Legends of the Comstock Lode*, Lucius Beebe and Charles Clegg present a photograph of that painting that was on display in one of the Virginia

Is this the real Julia Bulette? This Julia Bulette painting is at the Bucket of Blood Saloon. Note the red light to the right of Julia. *Photo by Bill Oberding.*

City saloons. They stated that this was the only known photo of Julia Bulette in existence and might or might not have been her. Certainly, we will never know—and perhaps this is the way Julia would have wanted it.

Julia was last seen alive on January 19 when she was turned away from Pipers Opera House for refusing to sit in the box assigned to ladies of her profession. The play she missed that evening was entitled *Willful Murder.* Being turned away from the city's top entertainment venue for such a ridiculous reason must have been difficult for Julia. She may have even told her close friend and neighbor Gertrude Holmes about the incident when they talked briefly that night. On the morning of January 20, the distraught Gertrude could remember very little of their last conversation. The sight of Julia's badly battered body was still too fresh in her mind. In time, the memory of it would fade, but not on this day. Gertrude had tried to rouse her friend for breakfast; now she forced her mind to forget that terrible scene and recall that Julia had mentioned she was expecting a visitor later that night. Since women of their profession never told others the names of their customers, Gertrude had no idea who that visitor had been.

At Police Chief Edwards's request, Gertrude made a quick search of Julia's belongings and noted that several items of clothing and jewelry were missing. Robbery was then determined to be the motive for Julia's murder. Some who lived in the vicinity thought they might have heard a woman's scream in the early morning hours. Gertrude had heard nothing. A coroner's inquest was conducted, and immediately afterward, Julia's funeral began. Because she was an honorary member of the Virginia City Engine Company No. 1, her funeral service was conducted at the firehouse on B Street. Reverend William M. Martin kindly gave a suitable eulogy for the slain woman, who was then given a send off the likes of which the city had never seen before or since. Of Julia, the *Territorial Enterprise* said, "In her lonely grave her good or bad traits alike lie buried with her."

Snow had fallen off and on all night long, yet a loyal crowd gathered in the light snow to say goodbye to Julia. The official funeral cortege included more than a dozen coaches draped in mourning; inside them, Julia's friends and acquaintances huddled together for warmth on this bone-chilling day.

As the coaches slipped and slid their way through the muddy streets, the Metropolitan Brass Band shuffled along playing a mournful dirge while members of Engine Company No. 1, outfitted in full regalia, followed on the sidewalks. Julia deserved this final show of respect.

The cortege wound its way through Virginia City and up toward Flowery Hill, where the coffin was solemnly lowered into the ground. Thus Julia was sent to her maker. Or was she? It's been well over one hundred years since that day, and yet mystery still surrounds Julia's final resting place.

A ghostly woman and a child have been seen in that certain spot on Flowery Hill where Julia is said to have been buried. This area has been pointed out to curious tourists as Julia Bulette's grave. However, there are some residents of Virginia City who believe the truth of her burial is somewhat more sordid.

The story is that an undertaker who prepared her for burial was enamored of the attractive Julia. He couldn't bear the thought of her being buried out on Flowery Hill, so he filled an empty coffin with sand and rocks and sent it on its way to the cemetery. Then, to keep Julia ever near, he buried her in his basement.

Julia's ghost, say those who have seen her, is still there, happily wandering through the building. A former owner of this building encountered the ghostly Julia early one summer morning. It was still too early for tourists to be out and about on the boardwalk, so she decided to give the three glass counters in her shop a good cleaning.

She was halfway through the job when she noticed a tall woman standing in the far corner of the store. Acknowledging the woman, the shop owner apologized for not seeing her sooner.

"Is there anything I can help you find?" she asked, noticing that the woman seemed to be looking around intently.

Suddenly the air turned icy, and the shop owner gasped as the woman in the corner slowly vanished into thin air. Later, she would say it was the apparition of Julia Bulette she saw in her shop that morning. The ghostly Julia may well haunt the upstairs portion of this building, but it is doubtful she was buried in its basement.

Most sightings of Julia occur late at night, including at the site where her little house stood at Union and D Streets and the isolated spot out on Flowery Hill where her lonely grave may or may not be located.

JOHN MILLIAN IS HANGED

A short distance from Geiger Grade, a large canyon forms a natural amphitheater. This is the location of John Millian's 1868 hanging for the murder of Virginia City courtesan Julia Bulette. Did I mention that this area is haunted?

Since the day of his execution, historians have pondered whether Millian was the actual killer or merely an unfortunate scapegoat. Even though he was caught with the dead woman's furs and jewelry in his possession, Millian maintained his innocence, insisting he had merely been the lookout for the actual killers. His case went to the Nevada Supreme Court, which upheld the conviction. Nothing more could be done for the young Frenchman. After his execution, Millian's attorney, Charles DeLong, presented a confession in which he denied the actual killing but admitted to unknowingly aiding the killers by standing watch for them.

A holiday atmosphere pervaded the crowd of nearly five thousand who had come to the canyon to witness the doomed man's demise. In attendance that morning were Mark Twain, who was in town to give a lecture at Piper's, and Comstock journalist Alfred Doten.

The men of the Comstock had thought highly of Julia and cheerfully celebrated the execution, while many of the women in attendance openly wept as the handsome Millian mounted the steps toward eternity. Since they had little use for Julia and her kind, the ladies had taken pity on the young convicted murderer, even going so far as to bake him sweets while he sat in the city jail awaiting his trip to the gallows.

Father Manogue accompanied Millian to his execution site, solemnly gave the killer his last rites and stepped back. According to a newspaper account, Millian then calmly addressed the crowd in French.

People of Virginia City; Today, the 24th of April at 1 o'clock, P.M., I ascend the scaffold to atone for a crime imputed to me. It is true that I do not consider myself as an honest man, but if I had had the chance of being

Fragment of rope used to hang John Millian,
the murderer of Julia Bulette, Virginia City,
April 24, 1868

Fragment of rope used to hang John Millian at the Nevada Capitol. *Photo by Bill Oberding.*

judged in any other country than Virginia, I would not have, I think, the pain of ending my life as odiously as I am about to end it.

Admitting that I deserve punishment, justice was not done to me. I have been treated as a stranger, in all cases; but in France it is for the stranger that we have the most regard. But, France is France, and all countries are not like France! In the country of France when a stranger finds himself in a position like that in which I found myself last year, we at first bring to him a person who speaks the language of his country correctly in order that he may not compromise himself—but here nothing of all that.

I was made to appear before the Chief of Police, who put question after question to me in order to be able to embarrass me in my answers, and that without knowing if I spoke the language of the country correctly (yes or no) and after that he nearly forced me to tell him that I was guilty. And then on my trial he swore false; but that does not regard me—it regards his conscience. May God forgive him, as I have forgiven him myself.

Then my lawyer had or had not the intention to save me. He flattered himself that he had my confession—that I had admitted all—then he had the intention to lose for me. That and the false swearing of the Chief of Police were the only causes of my condemnation, I believe.

My lawyer also refused to sign the petition that some charitable persons wanted to get up, to get my sentence commuted to the State prison—then he was not inclined to save my life. But Mr. DeLong is an American, and that is a great deal to consider. The people were greatly excited and I am a Frenchman. And in hanging me they thought to hang the whole of France; but they are mistaken for France will not be dishonored, for I am an American citizen. The fates were against me. I had no money, although my lawyer said that he wanted to take my case for nothing. It is more than probably [sic] that if I had had money I would not be reduced to mount the scaffold today. After all, in hanging me they do not hang the French people.

On my trial there came seven, or eight public women, who contributed greatly to my condemnation by their pretentious looks[,] their popularity in the country and by their impression on all the people. In another country those things are not permitted, but in Virginia City it is different; the public women are more respected than the honest ladies. It is true that this is seen only in the State of California and Nevada. I am going to die upon the scaffold, and that is a great shame for my family, who actually reside in France. But I find that God has a great deal of regard for me, for he gave me time to reconcile myself with him for my past faults, and done me a great favor because he did not permit me to leave the world in the miserable state that I had lived in for a long time. I hope that He will be more favorable to me than the justice of men. And if I have the chance of happiness to find grace in His Divine Majesty my lot is more to be envied that it appears. I profit by this occasion to thank from the bottom of my heart the good and charitable Sisters of St. Vincent de Paul; also the generous young ladies who offered their Holy Communion this morning for the repose of my soul.

I thank the Ladies of Virginia City who came to see me in my cell, and brought with them those consolations that only they could find in the circumstances. I entertain sentiments of thankfulness for the persons French, American and Canadian who made all the offers possible to save my life. They did not succeed but I thank them the same as if they had succeeded entirely.

O Holy ladies and Sisters of Charity, may the Lord reward you as you deserve for me. I am, with sentiments of most profound gratitude, your miserable servant. This is the confession that the people of Virginia and San Francisco have waited so long for. Done in my cell this 23rd day of April, 1868, eve of my execution.

Of the execution, Alfred Doten wrote, "Just as the black cap was drawn down over his head, the spring was touched, the trap dropped, and John

Millian dangled in the air. He fell about six feet. After about two minutes suspension a strong shudder pervaded his frame, otherwise he hung pretty quiet. At the expiration of 13 minutes all pulsation ceased to be apparent to the physicians."

Mark Twain was more graphic. After the execution, he wrote the following article, which appeared in the *Chicago Republican* issue of May 31, 1868:

Curious Changes
Special Correspondence of the Chicago Republican
Virginia, Nevada, May 2

I find some changes since I was here last. The little wildcat mines are abandoned and forgotten, and the happy millionaires in fancy (I used to be one of them) have wandered penniless to other climes, or have returned to honest labor for degrading wages. But the majority of the great silver mines on the Comstock lode are flourishing...

Novel Entertainment
But I am tired talking about mines. I saw a man hanged the other day. John Melanie [sic], of France. He was the first man ever hanged in this city (or country either), where the first twenty six graves in the cemetery were those of men who died by shots and stabs.

I never had witnessed an execution before, and did not believe I could be present at this one without turning away my head at the last moment. But I did not know what fascination there was about the thing, then. I only went because I thought I ought to have a lesson, and because I believed that if ever it would be possible to see a man hanged, and derive satisfaction from the spectacle, this was the time. For John Melanie was no common murderer—else he would have gone free. He was a heartless assassin.

A year ago, he secreted himself under the house of a woman of the town who lived alone, and in the dead watches of the night, he entered her room, knocked her senseless with a billet of wood as she slept, and then strangled her with his fingers. He carried off all her money, her watches, and every article of her wearing apparel, and the next day, with quiet effrontery, put some crepe on his arm and walked in her funeral procession.

Afterward he secreted himself under the bed of another woman of the town, and in the middle of the night was crawling out with a slung-shot in one hand and a butcher knife in the other, when the woman discovered him, alarmed the neighborhood with her screams, and he retreated from the house.

Melanie sold dresses and jewelry here and there until some of the articles were identified as belonging to the murdered courtezan. He was arrested and then his later intended victim recognized him.

After he was tried and condemned to death, he used to curse and swear at all who approached him; and he once grossly insulted some young Sisters of Charity who came to minister kindly to his wants. The morning of the execution, he joked with the barber, and told him not to cut his throat—he wanted the distinction of being hanged.

This is the man I wanted to see hung. I joined the appointed physicians, so that I might be admitted within the charmed circle and be close to Melanie. Now I never more shall be surprised at anything. That assassin got out of the closed carriage, and the first thing his eye fell upon was that awful gallows towering above a great sea of human heads, out yonder on the hill side and his cheek never blanched, and never a muscle quivered! He strode firmly away, and skipped gaily up the steps of the gallows like a happy girl. He looked around upon the people, calmly; he examined the gallows with a critical eye, and with the pleased curiosity of a man who sees for the first time a wonder he has often heard of. He swallowed frequently, but there was no evidence of trepidation about him—and not the slightest air of braggadocio whatever.

He prayed with the priest, and then drew out an abusive manuscript and read from it in a clear, strong voice, without a quaver in it. It was a broad, thin sheet of paper, and he held it apart in front of him as he stood. If ever his hand trembled in even the slightest degree, it never quivered that paper. I watched him at that sickening moment when the sheriff was fitting the noose about his neck, and pushing the knot this way and that to get it nicely adjusted to the hollow under his ear—and if they had been measuring Melanie for a shirt, he could not have been more perfectly serene. I never saw anything like that before. My own suspense was almost unbearable— my blood was leaping through my veins, and my thoughts were crowding and trampling upon each other. Twenty moments to live—fifteen to live— ten to live—five—three—heaven and earth, how the time galloped!—and yet that man stood there unmoved though he knew that the sheriff was reaching deliberately for the drop while the black cap descended over his quiet face!—then down through the hole in the scaffold the strap-bound figure shot like a dart!—a dreadful shiver started at the shoulders, violently convulsed the whole body all the way down, and died away with a tense drawing of the toes downward, like a doubled fist—and all was over!

I saw it all. I took exact note of every detail, even to Melanie's considerately helping to fix the leather strap that bound his legs together and his quiet removal of his slippers—and I never wish to see it again. I can see that stiff, straight corpse hanging there yet, with its black pillow-cased head turned rigidly to one side, and the purple streaks creeping through the hands and driving the fleshy hue of life before them. Ugh!

If there is any doubt of Millian's guilt, and if we accept the commonly held believe that ghosts occur because of injustice or unfinished business, we can readily understand why the ghostly Millian roams this lonely area where he was hanged so long ago.

HE OWNED A RESTAURANT

Virginia City locals may remember him. He owned a C Street restaurant for many years and was a creature of habit who rose early every morning and headed off to work just as the sun was rising over the Comstock. Those who knew him joked that you could set your clock by him as he could always be seen at the same time walking from his A Street home down Union Street toward his C Street restaurant. No matter the weather or what was going on in the world, this was his routine, and it never wavered.

Naturally, this dedication paid off. His restaurant was one of VC's most popular eateries. The décor was that of a bygone era, with lighting provided by antique crystal globes, walls covered in flocked crimson wallpaper and velvet drapes on the windows. The restaurant had all this elegance and a menu that listed several sumptuous dishes, reasonably priced.

The years went by. His gait grew slower, but he continued his morning ritual. Eventually, time caught up with him. He grew old and tired and no longer had the strength to walk up and down the steep hill.

He had been dead several years when a friend of his happened to be out on the streets at dawn. Imagine the man's shock when he saw his long-dead friend walking down Union Street. Some ghosts are interactive—that is, they communicate with the living. This wasn't the case; there was no interaction. The ghostly man walked as if in a trance, caught up in a never-ending event that played over and over in the environment he knew so well in life.

Paranormal researchers call this phenomena residual hauntings or place memories. Not exactly a ghost, but more like a scene from a movie being played over and over. It's possible that by his routine of many years, he has somehow left an impression of himself that replays on these streets.

Six-Mile Canyon

It's rumored that good-for-nothing stagecoach robber Jack Davis buried a cache of stolen loot somewhere in Six-Mile Canyon. Davis pretended to be a well-respected Virginia City businessman, all the while robbing stagecoaches as they crossed Geiger Grade. It was a profitable sideline for Jack, but eventually the truth came to light and the villainous Davis stood trial for his crimes. Found guilty, he was sentenced to spend many years at the state prison in Carson City.

Behind bars, Jack saw the error of his ways and reformed. When he learned that a group of his fellow inmates was planning a daring prison break, he steadfastly refused to join them. And then, after thinking the matter over, he informed the prison authorities about the escape. The state was appreciative. For his valuable assistance, Jack was given a full pardon. It was his second chance. Unfortunately, old habits die hard. Before long, Jack was back to his ways. Dubbed a gentleman robber for his respectful treatment of female passengers, Davis nonetheless raised the wrath of Wells Fargo. He had to be stopped. Detectives were ready and waiting for him one afternoon when he and his partners attempted to rob yet another stagecoach. Jack was killed in the ensuing shootout. He died before he could tell anyone the location of his ill-gotten treasure out in the Six-Mile Canyon area.

To this day, it is said that the ghost of Jack Davis angrily watches over the spot. Treasure hunters, take warning. The ghostly Jack does not take kindly to anyone getting too near his secret hiding place. He has been known to raise quite a ruckus if anyone dares do so. It's his treasure, and he means to keep it that way.

The Red Camel

The ghostly Jack Davis isn't the only specter haunting Six-Mile Canyon. Drivers have seen a misty apparition wandering along the canyon road late at night for many years. Perhaps this phantom is that of a man who was robbed and murdered in the canyon so long ago. Then again, maybe he is just another ghostly miner in search of a silver lode of his own.

Ghosts also reside in some of the other canyons. In 1885, Dan De Quille wrote an article for a San Francisco newspaper that told of the ghost of the "Lost Frenchman." This ghost sounds a bit like that of Henry Comstock.

Doomed to spend eternity chopping away at rocks and reenacting his own death scene, the specter remains lost in his mine somewhere in the canyons. De Quille also wrote of an old miner who swore to anyone who would listen that his partner's ghost not only haunted their cabin but also a big boulder in the canyon.

Other canyon sightings have included the mysterious red camel. Stories of the red camel ghost have been told throughout the Southwest for years. Here on the Comstock, Mexican miners first told of *el camello fantasmal* (the ghostly camel). Apparently, the camel makes its way through the canyons and then climbs over the top of Mount Davidson on certain nights when a full moon is high in the sky. On the ghostly beast's back is a grinning skeleton. Some people believe that the camel's specter is one of the Bactrian camels that were brought to Nevada during the late 1800s. The U.S. Army had first imported dromedary (one hump) camels to haul materials. In the late 1800s, Bactrian (two hump) camels were brought to Nevada and used to haul salt and other supplies across the desert and up to Virginia City. The creatures were not suited to Nevada's rugged terrain. Comstockers didn't like the camels, which were considered hideously ugly and unfriendly, and besides, they scared horses. This led Virginia City to pass an ordinance banning camels from its street during the day.

In 1875, the Nevada legislature went further when it passed a bill outlawing the animals from all public roads. They needn't have bothered. Camel owners and handlers were slowly realizing that camels were too much trouble. With nothing left to gain from ownership of the exotic creatures, many owners cruelly set the animals free. Left to fend for themselves in the hostile desert, most of the camels perished quickly. Others wandered aimlessly through the canyons for years afterward. They may be there still, haunting the canyons around Virginia City.

THE GHOST OF PETER LARKIN

On the morning of January 19, 1877, the ghost of Dan Corcoran finally got revenge. The Comstock was slammed by a winter storm that dumped more than a foot of snow on the area. In the Storey County Jail, Peter Larkin prepared for his trip to the gallows. Larkin, who had served as chief of the Virginia Fire Department years before, was popular and well liked; up until the end, he had hoped for a commutation. When he realized it wasn't to be, the unfortunate man bravely accepted his fate. According to the testimony of Nellie Sayers, Peter Larkin had shot and killed Dan Corcoran out of a jealous rage. Larkin and Sayers had been lovers until Corcoran happened along. It was also a fact that Corcoran had been shot in the stomach at close range in Nellie's home. At first Nellie claimed that Corcoran was to blame for his own death, but then the ghostly Corcoran began to visit her. That's when Nellie recanted her earlier statements, putting the blame on Larkin. It seems the unhappy apparition of Dan Corcoran had visited her several times. In these visits, the ghostly Corcoran urged her to tell the truth concerning his untimely end. And so, she had.

Nellie, a denizen of the roughest area in Virginia City, had anything but a sterling reputation. One writer for the *Territorial Enterprise* referred to Nellie as "the worst specimen of femininity ever to crawl down C Street." Still, Larkin was handed a death sentence on her testimony. Several people thought the sentence was too harsh and unwarranted. Larkin, they argued, was being made an example for anyone who would disturb the city's peace with murder and mayhem.

Before being hanged, Peter Larkin gave the sheriff his final farewell letter, which was read aloud:

> *Friends and fellow citizens. In a few minutes my connections with earthly things will cease, and I will appear before my final judge, in whom I have implicit confidence, and am confident of meeting in heaven the one I loved most dearly on earth, though long since passed from this world…my mother. Do not imagine that the community is ridding themselves of a man bad at heart, for I know myself and I tell you now, that a nobler man in every instinct of nature never suffered such ignominious death. I can account for it only in one way, That it was so ordained that this should be my fate. Why I should have been singled out for one to suffer in such manner I cannot possible conceive, for during my whole life I have attempted, as far as my nature would allow me, to follow the golden rule, and do unto others as I would others do unto me; but then, whys and wherefores are not for me to understand, and I will leave the matter in mystery to be solved by wiser men. I have been imprisoned nearly eighteen months, and though broken down both physically and mentally, I have nothing to complain of. I am willing to die, and can say that there is one thing that helps to console me in these, my last moments. It is that never during my life did I ever see any human being suffer for any of the necessaries of life that I did not assist them as far as my means would allow me. Hoping that you may find*

some good traits in my character, to speak well of me when I am gone, and wishing you all happiness in this world and hoping to meet you in a better one, I bid you farewell.

After the sheriff had read his statement, Larkin looked around at the men in attendance and said, "Well gentlemen, I bid you all goodbye, hoping that we will all meet in a better world."

He then glanced toward the hangman and uttered his last words: "Do it nobly now."

So Larkin was hanged, and the ghostly Corcoran was appeased. Whether the specter of Corcoran continued to visit Nellie, we will never know. She died a few months after Larkin's execution. And what of the ghost of Peter Larkin? He's said to haunt that area in back of the Storey County Courthouse where he was hanged. Several people have caught a glimpse of a shadowy figure during the early pre-dawn hours. Debbie Bender, owner of the Bats in the Belfry Virginia City Ghost Tour, has said that it is not uncommon to take a group by the courthouse at night and hear what sounds like wood slapping against wood (like a gallows). Bender told of an experience in the area while filming a late-night news special on ghosts in which recorders caught the sound of what seemed to be a hanging.

GHOST TABBY

Here kitty, kitty. When you talk to the locals in Virginia City, you'll soon hear about the town's ubiquitous ghost tabby. This yellow-gold kitty seems to be everywhere. The feline hangs out in shop doorways, at some of the saloons and has even been spotted strolling down the boardwalk. There are those who step over the tabby, and others who apparently don't see the ghostly cat and walk right through it. Some of the homes in town were built during or shortly after the Comstock boom. One in particular is most interesting. You see, it happens to be the residence of yet another ghostly kitty. Over the years, visitors to the home have told of hearing the purrs and soft meows of an invisible cat. Some have even felt the friendly feline brush up against them.

SUICIDE AND THE CITY

Life in early Virginia City was anything but easy. Suicide often seemed the only out. Suicide always leaves unanswered questions and unresolved issues in its wake. This is why some people believe that the act itself accounts for a number of hauntings. A person may regret his or her rash decision and choose to stay on this plane until the problems that led to suicide are finally faced and resolved. This could be a very long time. An example of this is the ghostly young prostitute in the Silver Queen. Does she stick around, wishing she'd made a different decision? I don't know of any studies on the suicide rate of the early Comstock. If any study exists or will be done in the future, it may show the suicide rate of that time (1860–1900) to be well above the national average of the same period.

Problems with love often resulted in suicide. E.F. Glover of American Flat was a member of the First Nevada State Legislature. The politician hardly seemed the type to end it all over a love affair gone sour, but he did just that on May 8, 1866. Glover went to the Tahoe House with three derringers and a plan. Once in his room, he removed his boots, sprawled on the bed and put a bullet in his heart. His note claimed he was leaving for the land from which no one returns because of a woman.

No one returns? He might have been wrong about that. Many of Virginia City's most haunted shops are housed in the building that was once the Tahoe House.

A spat with her husband over child rearing led Mrs. Henry Dods to drink strychnine. Being a dutiful wife, she prepared her husband's meal before ending it all.

In another case, when James R. McKay got tired of arguing religion with his wife, he went down into the family's wood cellar and severed his jugular vein.

Maria James was a young wife and mother living in Gold Hill. It may have been a spat with her husband, Zephaniah James, that led her to hang herself in the family's outhouse on a warm April evening.

The object of Fred Boegle's affection didn't return his feelings. Knowing that he couldn't live without the young lady, Boegle crawled under the railroad trestle bridge and sadly sipped his strychnine. By the time he was discovered, it was too late to save the twenty-something young man.

Loneliness and financial woes also led to suicide. Another hot summer was fast approaching, a time for families and picnics. But Widow Hoskins had no one. Feeling alone and forgotten, the old woman slit her own throat.

Six days before Christmas in 1893, Ernest Werrin died by his own hand—an overdose of morphine. Perhaps he suffered from the holiday blues long before there were malls, credit cards and ad campaigns with their portrayals of the idyllic Christmas season.

In September 1871, everything was crashing down on Justice William Livingston. The county commissioners were examining his books, and his greedy mistress wanted more money. He was a ruined man. In a fit of despondency, Justice Livingston went to his C Street office and ended it all with morphine.

The brothels on D Street were popular with many of Virginia City's male citizens, but they offered nothing more than temporary shelter and a decent meal for the women who worked in them. As youth vanished, a woman was usually shown the door in such establishments. With no other prospects, many of them chose to put an end to their problems with morphine, a drink of strychnine or laudanum.

Age wasn't necessarily a factor in prostitute suicides. Unwanted pregnancies and failed love affairs were the reasons many younger women chose suicide as an escape from the life fate had cast them in.

Some deaths that were labeled suicides may have been the results of accidents or undiagnosed illnesses. While it's likely most recorded suicides were just that, another possibility does exist. In the days before fingerprints, death scene analysis, DNA and forensic specialists, suicide could have easily been used as a cover-up for murder.

Ghost Adventures Live Ghost Hunt Takes to the Basement

When the show first started out, *Ghost Adventures* did two live ghost hunts: one in Goldfield and the other here in Virginia City. It was during the live ghost hunt in Virginia City that a group of investigators converged in the darkened basement of the Mark Twain Book Store, which was housed in the Colonel Morris Pinschower Building. Since it was built in 1862, the building has been used as Joseph Frederick Hardware, the Nevada Bank of San Francisco, a livery stable, a garage and a car dealership.

On this night, the focus was the gnome-like statue in one corner, the eerie, grinning Tommyknocker. According to Cornish folklore, Tommyknockers were elves that followed men into the mines. While they could be kindness itself, these imps usually enjoyed being mischievous. They were said to warn

Tommyknocker statue. *Photo by Bill Oberding.*

miners with loud knocking just before a cave in, but Tommyknockers also hid tools, and switched lunch pails.

They were not really bad creatures, but on this particular night, some investigators complained of intense feelings while photographing the Tommyknocker statue. Do his eyes really follow as people move about the basement? Some insist they do.

Once everyone had moved past the Tommyknocker, all the lights were turned off. Now the basement was as black as Count Dracula's cape. Even with an occasional light blast from digital cameras and meters, we were surrounded by darkness. Psychic impressions included a carriage and a small child. This may not be as strange as it sounds, considering the livery stable that once stood here. Remnants of horse stalls remain. There is also the rumor that skeletal human remains were discovered in the basement at one time.

Those of us with digital recorders quietly coaxed the ghost to speak into them. On playback much later, I heard a whispered word: "Anger."

Did this mean someone was angry down in the basement? I listened to that one word again and again. What did it mean? Who was angry? These are questions that will likely never be answered.

Our session over, we headed up the stairs, each of us careful not to brush against the Tommyknocker. The next group that descended the stairs that night consisted of several people who were interested in buying the creepy little Tommyknocker and taking him home. No deal. Owner Joe Curtis would not sell him.

THE WASHOE SEERESS

Eilley Bowers was fascinated with ghosts and the afterlife. Using her peep stone (crystal ball), Eilley had the uncanny ability to tap into the spiritual realm. The subject of some derision, she was dubbed the "Washoe Seeress," and Dan De Quille (the pen name of William Wright) referred to her that way in his book *The Big Bonanza*. A remarkable woman with the ability to persevere in a world that wasn't always accepting of her and her eccentricities, Eilley is as much a part of Comstock history as John Mackay, Julia Bulette and Mark Twain.

The untimely death of her husband, Sandy, left Eilley heartbroken and penniless. When creditors began hounding her for payment, Eilley sold her precious belongings, one by one. Still it wasn't enough to cover the mountain of debts Sandy had so carelessly left behind.

A resourceful woman, she used her interest in the spirit world as a means of feeding herself and her daughter, Persia. She'd always consulted her peep stone in matters of importance in her life; now Eilley gazed into it and claimed to be able to foretell the future and communicate with the dead.

In an attempt to shield Persia from the problems at Bowers Mansion, Eilley sent her to school in Reno. The little girl flourished in the city, and Eilley allowed herself to believe that life would soon be better for them. But it wasn't to be. The couple with whom Persia boarded sent word that the child was gravely ill. Eilley frantically tried to get to daughter her in time, but she was too late. The death of her only child changed Eilley. Those who knew her best said the heavy grief of losing first Sandy and then Persia was the undoing of Eilley's mind.

Eventually Eilley came to trust the dead more than the living. Those in the spirit realm had never disappointed her the way some in this world had. As she grew older and lonelier, she sought solace hunched over her peep stone and conversing with the dearly departed.

The spirits helped her with the guidance she happily dispensed to the townspeople of Virginia City and Reno. While others questioned some of the far-fetched things Eilley saw in the depths of her crystal ball, she never questioned the spirits; they had spoken, and that was enough for her.

Though she spent her later years in northern California, Eilley visited Virginia City as often as she could. She came to enjoy the companionship of a dear friend and to bask in her notoriety as the Washoe Seeress.

Eilley knew better than to expect much quiet time while visiting in her friend's home on C Street. The two old ladies sat in the parlor and reminisced about their early days in Gold Hill, knowing that the *Territorial Enterprise* would eventually announce her arrival on the Comstock. As soon as the newspaper hit the streets, those in need of Eilley's spiritual guidance besieged her with their problems.

Some came to her in the hopes of striking it rich with a new mining claim. Others consulted with her about more practical matters. One evening just as the moon was rising over Mount Davidson, a young man came to ask her assistance in finding his stolen bag of gold dust. Ever prepared to see that evildoers paid for their misdeeds, Eilley agreed to help. She sat down, stared into the peep stone for what seemed an eternity and then calmly announced the name of the culprit. Further, she told the man exactly where the thief was hiding out in Six-Mile Canyon.

The young man angrily lit out. When he found the crook and his bag of gold dust, he gave the thief a beating he wouldn't soon forget and raced back to the saloon with news of Eilley's remarkable powers.

Another of her cases involved a missing ring. The sparkler held much sentimental value for its owner, who was grief-stricken at having so carelessly lost it. A large reward was offered, but still the ring was nowhere to be found. In desperation, it was decided to call in the Washoe Seeress. Eilley peered deep into her crystal ball and accurately predicted there was no need for concern, as the ring would ultimately be returned. Within a week, the ring was once more in the owner's possession.

The Washoe Seeress was consulted for help in locating mines that were rich in ore. However, if anyone became wealthy from her direction, they chose to remain silent on the matter. She may have been the butt of cruel jokes, but still Eilley's help was often requested in matters of life and death. When miners became trapped in mines far below the city, she was called in as a last resort. Occasionally she was successful in helping to save men from certain death.

It wasn't only the living who sought Eilley's assistance on matters of importance. One spring evening in 1878, the spirit of Joe, a man who lay buried in an unmarked grave on Virginia City's Cemetery Hill, contacted her, according to the *Territorial Enterprise*. Apparently, Joe was not resting peacefully.

He only wanted someone to be so kind as to determine the exact location of his grave. To do this, one merely had to ask the undertaker just where he'd buried Joe. Then flowers and remembrances could be placed on his grave. The spirit of Joe is quoted as having told Eilley, "If you could see the thousands of disembodied spirits hovering over the cemetery on that occasion, you would feel amply repaid for your trouble."

In Reno, Eilley opened a small fortunetelling and séance business for a while. Not one to mince words, she soon incurred some of that town's wrath when she told a well-heeled businessman that his time on earth was just about over. Apparently it was more information than the gentleman needed to know. Eilley couldn't understand this. Wasn't it far better to know these things, she reasoned.

While living in Reno, Eilley communicated with a man by the name of Joseph Rover. Rover had been hanged in that city for the murder of his business partner, and Eilley was a sympathetic listener. Soon his spirit was visiting regularly with her. On these occasions, Rover invariably maintained his innocence of the crime that had sent him to the gallows.

Eilley believed him and told her friends about Mr. Rover's insistence that he'd done nothing wrong. But she was alone in her belief that the spirit spoke the truth. Some twenty years later, another man made a startling deathbed confession when he claimed that it was he, and not Joseph Rover, who had killed their business partner, Mr. Sharp, in the Black Rock Desert.

Using her gift of second sight, Eilley was able to help many people, some of whom were quite eager to share their experiences with others. On May 10, 1878, the following article appeared in the *Territorial Enterprise*:

> *DOINGS OF THE "WASHOE SEERESS"*
> *Mrs. E.L. Hickox, the well-known milliner, No. 138 South C Street, sends us the following note; "I write you a few lines in regard to the insurance policy which I advertised in the ENTERPRISE a few weeks ago. Shortly after I advertised I was advised to go to Mrs. Bowers, the "Washoe Seeress," but I had no faith in spirit communications, and delayed going until a few days since, then went more out of curiosity than anything else. Mrs. Bowers told me that whatever it was that I had lost was in a large envelope and had been stolen by a woman. Furthermore, she went on and described a lady that I was sure had been in my store the day I missed the paper. She then told me how to proceed to recover my property. I followed her directions, and am happy to say found my lost policy, and the woman who took it apologized in a very humble manner and promised to pay me the money that was taken at the same time. I think it my duty to make this known through the columns of the ENTERPRISE. I am willing to go before a Notary Public, if necessary, and make affidavit to what I have stated above.*

The Crown Point Prophesy

Eilley Bowers was not shy about sharing her prophecies with others. If she saw it in the peep stone, she told it. But she was innocent of a cruel prophecy that was somehow attributed to her in early spring of 1878.

The Storey County School District had decided on a picnic in Carson City. A gala event of music, dancing, laughter and food, the picnic was to be an all-day affair. Plans were made, and as the picnic day approached, people on the Comstock talked of little else—until the rumors started to circulate and frighten them. Supposedly, the Washoe Seeress had predicted that the Crown Point Bridge would be destroyed on the day of the picnic as the trains rolled across it on their way to Carson City.

Finally, the day of the picnic arrived. Across the canyons, the sun was barely beginning to creep over the horizon. The sky was cloudless and blue. It looked like a fine day for an outing. Eight train cars filled with excited passengers rolled out of the Virginia City and Gold Hill depots. Determined to show her support, Eilley was among the more than two thousand passengers who rode the trains that day. It was her way of disproving the frightening rumor that had circulated through Virginia City and Gold Hill.

Angered at the fear the rumor had generated, she took out the following ad in a June 1878 edition of the *Territorial Enterprise*:

> *Having been informed that certain maliciously disposed persons are circulating a report that I have predicted that an accident would befall the school picnic party on Saturday next by the breaking down of the Crown Point ravine railroad bridge, I desire in this public manner to state that the report is false in every particular. On the contrary, I am under the impression that the coming picnic excursion will be one of the pleasantest of the season. Mrs. A. Bowers.*

Another ad appeared in the *Territorial Enterprise* under "Personals" on June 10, 1878, that read:

> *Mrs. S.L. Bowers, the Washoe Seeress attended the picnic of the school children yesterday. It was reported that Mrs. Bowers had predicted that the Crown Point Bridge would break down while the excursion train was passing over it, therefore she went on the train to show that she was confident that no such accident would occur.*

Ridicule and poverty marred Eilley's last years. Just as she'd predicted so many years before, her finances had come full circle. Eilley, who'd risen from washing clothes in Johnstown to become one of the wealthiest women in Nevada, died penniless and alone in her tiny room at the Daughters of Kings Charitable Home for Women in Oakland, California, on October 27, 1903.

The kindhearted new owner of Bowers Mansion, Henry Riter, paid to have George Gilloghy pick up her ashes at an Oakland crematory and bring them back to Nevada. A Reno newspaper described her return trip: "All that is mortal of Mrs. Sandy Bowers will be brought up from the west next Sunday morning and transferred to the Virginia Truckee Railroad."

Eilley came home to Washoe Valley, and there she was buried beside her beloved Sandy and Persia on a hill that overlooks their home, Bowers Mansion. And so she rests—or does she?

SUPERSTITIOUS MINERS

The mines are still there, far beneath Virginia City. They may be empty, but they aren't necessarily silent. In the quiet pre-dawn hours, some Virginia City residents will tell you that it's possible to still hear the pitiful moans and terror-filled cries of those unfortunate miners who lost their lives in the mines so long ago. Men worked the long, grueling hours of their shifts under the constant threat of death. Noxious gases, boiling water and fire were dangers miners faced daily. Working in the mines was a dangerous occupation. One stroll through the Silver Terrace Cemetery attests to that.

Accidents were a constant of a miner's life, and so was superstition. This helped to keep a man diligent and safe. An example of such superstition is the story of the lucky miner who happened to be riding to work with some co-workers one morning when a ghostly man darted out in front of their wagon. The specter stopped and smiled sadly at the men before it ran to the other side of the street and quickly dissolved into thin air. The horses were so startled that it took the driver several minutes to calm the terrified animals. The lucky miner was more scared than he'd ever been in his life. Telling himself that the ghost had been an omen of impending death, he jumped from the wagon, refusing to go farther. Today, he was certain, danger waited in the mine. The other miners, apparently not as superstitious as he, laughed uproariously at his fear. But he steadfastly insisted that to go to the mine that day meant certain death. He was right. That very afternoon there was a terrible cave in at the mine, and all those who'd been in the wagon with him perished.

Superstition like this was rampant. If it might save his life, a miner wouldn't usually make light of another's superstition. So it was. A miner would not work if he'd seen a redheaded woman on his way to work. Like the superstition of women on sailing ships, this meant certain doom. Cornish miners believed in the Tommyknockers, elf-like creatures that could either help or hinder a man's chances for survival while deep within the earth.

Each time he descended into the mine, a man knew that he might never come back up—alive, at least. If he was lucky enough to escape the dangers that threatened his life, he still faced the threat of being grotesquely mangled by faulty equipment or falling debris. Fire was the most perilous threat of all.

Early on the morning of April 7, 1869, warning whistles sounded. A fire was raging in the Yellow Jacket Mine near the eight-hundred-foot level. Tall billows of smoke poured from the shaft of the Yellow Jacket and those of the nearby Kentuck and Crown Point Mines. The Yellow Jacket fire was one of the worst mine disasters in Virginia City's history. Wives and family members rushed to the site in hopes that their loved ones would be spared. One after another, burnt corpses were pulled from the mines. Some had been so badly mangled that they were beyond all recognition. In describing the condition of the bodies, Alf Doten wrote, "Some 3 or 4 I saw at the undertakers had heads crushed horribly—one had his head torn entirely off." Undertakers' parlors filled with the bodies of the luckless miners who'd met their end in the Yellow Jacket Mine disaster. In all, thirty-seven miners lost their lives in the fire.

While the towns of Virginia City and Gold Hill mourned the deaths, work in the mines continued—and so did the accidents. On June 18, 1880, an ore car loaded with tools and other equipment fell, killing five men and injuring many others at the Yellow Jacket Mine.

These were certainly not the only such tragedies to occur on the Comstock. In the early evening hours of June 24, 1887, fire was discovered at the 1,500-foot level of the Gould and Curry Mine. All but eleven miners escaped with their lives. Five men attempted to get out by way of an old tunnel that was no longer in use. They died after being overcome by noxious smoke and gases. Another group of miners was trapped deep within the tunnel. One after another, rescue attempts failed. By July 9, all hope was gone. The next day, the lifeless bodies of the six miners who'd been entombed in the mine were brought to the surface. No one was safe in the mines—in the spring of 1864, an accident at the Chollar Mine took the life of Joseph Rassett, a Chollar Company trustee, when he fell more than fifty feet down the shaft.

Workplace violence also took place in the mines; such is the case of Pat Crowley, who killed his shift supervisor, William Nichols, at the Savage Mine in July 1890. After battering the unfortunate Nichols's head in with a pickaxe, Crowley claimed that the dead man had called him vile names. He then gave himself up to authorities without resistance.

THE TRAGEDY OF THE JONES BOYS

Everyone knows that cemeteries are haunted, but there's got to be a good reason for a ghost to stay in the cemetery when there are so many other places to haunt. In the case of the Jones boys who haunt the Gold Hill Cemetery, it's probably the freedom to enjoy themselves, which they never knew in their short lives.

On Christmas Eve in 1871, a blizzard blew in from the mountains, blanketing the Comstock with heavy snow. American Flat rancher Bob Jones noticed that one of his calves had wandered off and cruelly sent his sons Henry and John out into the snowstorm in search of it. A harsh disciplinarian, Jones warned the boys not to come back without the animal. Having suffered his abuse before, they knew better than to return empty-handed. While others spent their Christmas Eve celebrating with friends and family, the Jones boys spent the last hours of their lives looking for the errant calf.

Before we get angry at Bob Jones, let's look at another version of the tale that absolves him of some cruelty. In this story, he sent the boys to work at his other ranch. As Christmas drew near, he sent word for them to come home for the holiday. It was during their trek homeward in the blinding snowstorm that the boys got lost and froze to death.

Their bodies were found on the Ophir Grade. It was a sorrowful Christmastime for the people of the Comstock. News of the deaths only intensified people's dislike of Bob Jones. Whatever pain he may have felt over the loss of his sons, Jones wisely kept to himself.

Six months later, in June 1872, a local spiritualist/medium was conducting a séance when she went into a trance and received a message from the Jones boys. They were happy on the other side, happier than they had ever been in life. Over the years, there have been numerous sightings of Henry and John in the Gold Hill Cemetery, where they are buried. Those who've seen the ghosts say they do seem to be enjoying themselves in the afterlife.

Bob Jones eventually moved down to Reno, where he died on October 14, 1903. But this doesn't end the story of the Jones boys. Sometime after 1974, vandals, as they often do, decided to deface and destroy markers in the Gold Hill Cemetery. One of the markers that was stolen was that of Henry and John Jones. It would remain missing for forty years. But through a joint preservation project effort between the Bureau of Land Management and the Comstock Cemetery Foundation, the Jones boys' grave site was reconstructed and the old headstone returned.

Séances and Fortunetellers

Spiritualism, the belief that the dead can and do communicate with the living through mediums, started in 1848 with the Fox sisters, Kate and Margaret, of Hydesville, New York. The girls amazed their friends and neighbors with their ability to communicate with a spirit that resided in their haunted house. This was achieved by asking questions that the spirit would answer with knocks and raps. Word of the two girls' ability to converse with the spirit quickly spread, and interest grew. The public was intrigued with this new opportunity to communicate with the dead. Margaret and Kate Fox were called upon to give public demonstrations of their abilities, and enjoying their newfound fame, they gladly did so.

As popular in their day as famous psychics are today, spiritualists made regular stops throughout the country and in Nevada's mining towns. Entertaining and amazing people with their uncanny abilities, spiritualists like Mrs. Ada Hoyt Foye were able to command high ticket prices from those who attended their lectures and séances in Virginia City. And just as people do today with ghost hunting, societies and clubs were formed for those who were interested in spiritualism.

While the accuracy of these women's predictions couldn't always be counted on, one prediction does stand out. A month before the Great Fire of 1875, mediums warned that a fire would destroy Virginia City. In a time before TV, movies and social media, people turned to fortunetellers and séances as a means of entertainment. All these séances may be one reason that Virginia City is so haunted. Spirits were called upon for advice in matters of love and life. It's really not so difficult to believe that some may have decided to stay on in the city long after their assistance was sought.

The November 13, 1872 edition of the *Territorial Enterprise* reported on Agnes McDonough, a teenager who had been visited by the ghost of her father, dead six years. Agnes, who had lived with relatives for several years, carried on conversations with her father's spirit through knocks and raps. The incident aroused the attention of Father Manogue of St. Mary's and was reported in the *Catholic Guardian*.

Alfred Doten and the Dial

The dial, a precursor to the Ouija board, was a popular apparatus for communicating with the afterlife. In his journals, Doten wrote of "sitting at the dial." He claimed that his mother and father had both sent messages from beyond while he sat at the dial.

On November 3, 1867, Doten attended the funeral of his friend Mrs. Ordway. A few days later, he attended a séance given by the famed Mrs. Foye. At that time, Mrs. Ordway did not make an appearance. However, on the evening of October 18, 1868, Doten had been sitting at the dial for over an hour when she came through to him. Even though she had been dead nearly a year, Mrs. Ordway shared a secret with Doten—the true age of her husband's new wife—and lots of intelligent but unimportant communications.

Doten's fascination with séances, the dial and the spirit realm seems to have faded as he grew older. His later writings contain less on the subject.

Mark Twain on Séances

Speaking of the afterlife, Mark Twain said, "I am silent on the subject because of necessity. I have friends in both places."

Professor James Hyslop's 1919 *Contact with the Other World: the Latest Evidence as to Communication with the Dead* was a breakthrough work that purported to show research on spirits, the afterlife and cases of communication with famous people. One of these was Mark Twain, who, according to Hyslop, had dictated an entire book from the grave via the Ouija board. A change of heart perhaps, because in life, Twain had taken delight in pointing out the absurdities he found in beliefs of the supernatural. Hyslop pointed out Twain's incongruities by detailing the premonition Twain had concerning the death of his younger brother, Henry. Calling his premonition "Mental Telegraphy," Mark Twain wrote an article on it, but it was rejected by publishers who assumed it to be a joke. The following is an excerpt from an article Twain wrote for the February 1866 issue of the *Territorial Enterprise* on séances.

> I shall have this matter of spiritualism "down to a spot," yet, if I do not go crazy in the meantime.
>
> I stumbled upon a private fireside séance a night or two ago, where two old gentlemen and a middle-aged gentleman and his wife were communicating (as they firmly believed) with the ghosts of the departed. They have met for this purpose every week for years. They do not "investigate"—they have long since become strong believers, and further investigations are not needed by them. I knew some of these parties well enough to know that whatever deviltry was

exhibited would be honest, at least, and that if there were any humbugging done they themselves would be as badly humbugged as any spectator. We kept the investigations going for three hours, and it was rare fun.

They set a little table, in the middle of the floor, and set up a dial on it which bore the letters of the alphabet instead of the figures of a clock-face. An index like the minute hand of a clock was so arranged that the tipping of the table would cause it to move around the dial and point to any desired letter, and thus spell words. The lady and two gentlemen sat at the table and rested their hands gently upon it, no other portion of their persons touching it. And the spirits, and some other mysterious agency, came and tilted the table back and forth, sometimes lifting two of its legs three or four inches from the floor and causing the minute hand to travel entirely around the dial. These persons did not move the table themselves; because when no one's hands rested upon it but the lady's it tilted just the same, and although she could have borne down her side of the table, by an effort, it was impossible for her to lift up her side with her hands simply resting top of it. And then the hands of these persons lay perfectly impassable—not rose or fell, and not a tendon grew tense or relaxed as the table tilted—whereas, when they removed their hands and I tilted the table with mine, it required such exertion that muscles and tendons rose and fell and stretched and relaxed with every movement. I do not know who tilted that table, but it was not the medium at any rate. It tired my arms to death merely to spell out four long words on the dial, but the lady and the ghosts spelled out long conversations without the least fatigue. I think I ought to file a protest against some of the malevolent criticisms that have been made in my absence. Do you know how I have been hashed up since I died?

The first ghost that announced his presence spelled this on the dial: "My name is Thomas Tilson; I was a preacher. I have been dead many years. I know this man Mark Twain well!"

I involuntarily exclaimed: "The very devil you do?" That old dead parson took me by surprise when he spelled my name, and I felt the cold chills creep over me. Then the ghost and I continued the conversation:

"Did you know me on earth?"

"No. But I read what you write, every day, almost. I like your writings."

"Thank you. But how do you read it? Do they take the Territorial Enterprise in h____ or rather, in heaven, I beg your pardon?"

"No. I read it through my affinity."

"Who is your affinity?"

"Mac Crellish of the Alta!" [Note: the *Alta Almanac* was published every year by F. Mac Crellish & Company of San Francisco]

Pine Trees at the Firehouse Restaurant

He was homeless, down and out. Occasionally he would be seen foraging through garbage cans. Well liked in VC, even during an angry outburst, most people considered him harmless. And then came that day on C Street when he angrily confronted a tourist, frightening her and her child. The shopkeeper called a deputy sheriff. And out in front of the former Firehouse Restaurant, a tragic scene played out.

The homeless man held his knife and faced the deputy, slowly edging toward him. The deputy ordered him to drop the knife, to stop. He didn't. Instead, he made as if to lunge at the deputy, who fired off two shots. The homeless man died there on the sidewalk beside one of the boxed pine trees.

Months later, I was holding one of my first Virginia City conferences. A friend who claimed to be a very gifted sensitive was in town for the occasion. On one of our walks of the downtown area, I decided to test his abilities. We started walking up C Street. When we got to the spot where the homeless man had died, my friend stopped and grabbed his chest.

"Oh my God! I feel as if—as if I've been shot."

Forgetting about my psychic test, I asked. "Are you alright? Should we call 911?"

Tears were streaming down his face as he said, "No, I am fine. But someone…someone suffered a lot of pain and distress here."

At the time of the shooting, there were four boxed pine trees in front of this restaurant. Shortly after that incident, one of them turned yellow and died. This was the pine tree near the spot where the homeless man died. What does it mean? I can't explain *why* it happened, only say that it did.

All the trees have since been removed, and a new restaurant has moved in.

Motorcyclist on Geiger Grade

This story could well be urban legend, like that of the hitchhiking prom queen or the headless woman who roams country roads late at night. It may be the twenty-first-century version of the long-told tale of the ghostly stage going over the edge of Geiger Grade. Then again, it could be a cautionary tale for the thousands of bikers who converge on the Comstock during Reno's annual Street Vibration event. During this September event, a steady stream of motorcycles roar up the canyon to Virginia City. It is a long way down, and invariably there are accidents, some of them fatal. Still, many riders barely slow their bikes as they round the dangerous hairpin curves of Highway 341.

Imagine that it's dark. You've spent the day in Virginia City, and now you're driving back down Geiger Grade. In the rearview mirror, you see a single headlight glowing off in the distance, a motorcycle. You're observing the posted speed limit. The biker isn't. Suddenly, the unmistakable sound of a motorcycle is closing in on you. The headlight is too close. You pull over at the next turnout and wait for the motorcycle to fly past. But there is nothing. Only the darkness and the silence. Yours is the only vehicle on this stretch of Geiger Grade.

So where did the motorcycle go? Not over the canyon. A strange and unsettling experience to be sure, but there are those who claim this has occurred on Geiger Grade. Best advice should this happen to you? The turnouts are for slower vehicles to make way for those who choose to cruise at a higher rate of speed. Pull over at the next turnout and wait for the motorcycle to pass. Possibly, the rider is a living breathing person who only wants to get somewhere faster than you do. The other possibility is, of course, that you've just encountered the ghostly motorcyclist.

Walks Down D Street

There's an intriguing Virginia City tale of a long-ago hearse that occasionally makes its way down D Street toward the cemetery. Once at the cemetery, the hearse vanishes. Could this be the source of the ghostly coach noise in the following tale?

An impromptu investigation of the D Street area took place on a clear night on the Comstock. The sky was strewn with hundreds of sparkling stars that surrounded a sliver of moon. Bundled up against the cold, we walked the street in silence, taking photos and trying to collect EVP. It was late, and the town was silent.

Suddenly the silence was broken by the sound of horses' hooves and coach wheels grinding their way down the street. We stopped and listened until the sound slowly faded. As we expected, there was no one else on the street. We listened to our recordings carefully, but there were no discernable sounds that matched what we had heard. According to some, D Street is very active late at night. There are reports of raucous laughter and soft weeping that rises and then vanishes like the wind.

Another Walk, Another Time

It was well past midnight. Most people had long since gone to bed, but as ghost hunters, we stay up all hours. We were walking down D Street. Suddenly someone in the group asked, "Do you see that?" pointing toward the church.

We did. A glowing figure in the distance seemed to taunt us; with each step we took toward it, the apparition seemed to move one step farther from us. Who could it be?

"Hello there! We thought you were a ghost," I called.

I laughed nervously. How strange we must seem to this person. The figure turned away from us and dissolved—and when I say "dissolved," I mean the thing just seemed to drop down to the ground and disappear.

This apparition could be any number of long-ago residents. This area along D Street was the city's notorious red-light district, and many of the city's demimonde plied their trade here. Cad Thompson's Brick House and Jenny Tyler's Bow Windows were probably the most popular bordellos on the Comstock.

Though Cad Thompson and Jenny Tyler were said to be kind to their employees, life on D. Street was never easy. Many of the prostitutes turned to drugs, alcohol and eventually suicide when life got the better of them.

Such is the case of Ida Vernon, a young woman who became addicted to opium. Late in the morning of February 6, 1868, she was found dead in her bed at the Bow Windows brothel. Accidental overdose or intentional suicide—no one was really quite certain. Either way, Ida escaped her troubles.

The women who ran the brothels often led sad, tumultuous lives themselves. Many didn't fare any better than the woman who worked for them. Jessie Lester is an example. The wealthiest madam on the Comstock, Lester got into a heated argument on Christmas Eve 1864 that ended with her being shot. She steadfastly refused to divulge the name of her assailant, even when the amputation of her right arm became necessary. Lester lingered in agony for a month; when she died, the identity of the person who shot her was still a mystery. Many believed that a former boyfriend had shot Jessie when she refused to give him money to cover his enormous gambling debts. His name was just one of many mysteries she took to her grave in the Silver Terrace Cemetery.

Old Lady at the Gold Strike

Why is it that skeptics always seem to get the worst of it in their discovery of ghosts? A friend told me about her day trip to Virginia City with her skeptical boyfriend. They walked into the Gold Strike gift shop at 122 C Street, looking for after-season bargains. She recalled:

For some reason we felt compelled to go to the back of the shop where the fortuneteller's area is. It was quiet. No one was in the shop but the clerk and us.

"Look at that old woman," my boyfriend whispered, pointing toward an empty space.

I didn't see anything.

"Over there! She's looking right at us," he insisted.

My friend focused her eyes on the area, wondering if he was seeing a ghost. But she didn't see whatever it was that had him mesmerized.

"Must be a ghost," she chuckled.

"You must need your eyes checked," he said.

They bought a few items and walked out onto the boardwalk. Suddenly, he jumped back, saying, "Did you see that? That old lady just ran up and bopped me on the nose."

It was fun to see her skeptical boyfriend squirm. She couldn't help but laugh at his alarm. But she stopped laughing when she looked at his nose and saw a spot the size of a pinprick bleeding profusely.

The Faceless Phantom

Who is she? This faceless apparition has been frightening Comstock children ever since she first appeared at the corner of Carson and A Streets decades ago. Dressed in casual attire that's decidedly outdated, this ghost walks back and forth from the intersection of the two streets to a spot some blocks away. If there is a reason for her haunting this specific area, it could be that she or a loved one perished in the great fire of October 26, 1875.

The *Territorial Enterprise* of October 27, 1875, reported on the fire:

Virginia City in Ruins
A Fearful and Uncontrollable Conflagration—The Heart of the City
Swept Away—Several Thousand Persons Homeless—The Immediate
Loss Probably About $7,000,000—Consolidated Virginia Hoisting
Works and Mill, the Ophir Works and the New California Stamp Mill
Destroyed—But Little Property Saved Anywhere in the City.

Yesterday morning, at 5:30 o'clock, a fire broke out in a lodging-house on
A Street, about midway between Taylor and Union Streets, and nearly in
the rear of William Mooney's livery stable, and soon got beyond the control
of the Fire Department, when it swept through and destroyed nearly the
whole of the business part of the city. Before water was got on the fire
several wooden buildings adjoining the lodging house were on fire, and it
was plainly to be seen that a great fire was imminent.

A heavy wind was blowing from the west, and this veered about in all
directions as the fire increased in magnitude, firing buildings on all sides
with alarming rapidity. It was soon seen that the efforts of the firemen
to control the flames would be fruitless, and the people began to assert
themselves to save their goods. The wildest confusion prevailed, as all saw
that, exert themselves as they might, the rapidly advancing flames must soon
overwhelm their homes and household goods and gods.

Although the general course of the wind was from the west, yet the flames
rapidly backed up against it and also moved at great speed to the north and
south, while they rushed at race-horse speed to the eastward, making great
leaps from building to building [sic].

Those who've seen this ghost say that even though her face is completely indistinguishable, she is crying. They know this because the sound of soft weeping follows her. Perhaps she lost a loved one or property in the great fire and has never overcome her sorrow and remorse. But there is another theory. Some say she is a widow who died in the city some fifty years ago. Others insist on a more sinister explanation of the faceless phantom. They say she is the apparition of a woman who was born and raised in the city during the Roaring Twenties. Bored with life in the small town, she ran away to San Francisco, where she eventually married and settled down. Years later, her husband, a very successful businessman, murdered her out of love for another woman. Whoever she is, whatever her story may be, she's not content to stay in one spot. Occasionally she's spotted in other areas of town.

GHOST DOG OF D STREET

Virginia City seems to have its share of ghostly animals. And why not? I think it's only fair. If the ghosts of our fellow humans can return, animals should also have the privilege of haunting, and, of course, I believe that they do.

Anyone who has ever shared their home with a pet knows that they return our love tenfold. Ida and Earl had lived in Virginia City for nearly thirty years. Like many childless couples, they bestowed their parental love and affection on their pets. Over the years, they'd owned several dogs, but a little fox terrier by the name of Ruffles was the favorite. Earl and Ruffles were inseparable; wherever one went, so went the other.

Then came winter, and death claimed them within a week of each other. Earl died of a massive heart attack while chopping firewood in the backyard. On the day of Earl's funeral, Ruffles was hit and killed by a car. Ida consoled herself with the thought that the two of them were at least together. The years passed, old friends moved away or died and neighbors came and went. One morning, Ida, who was normally very reserved, stopped to chat at the back fence with a new neighbor about gardening.

"It's a wonder that little dog doesn't destroy your beautiful flower garden, the way he likes to wallow in it," the neighbor chuckled.

"What dog?" Ida asked.

"The little dog that wanders into your backyard sometimes. I've seen a man come to the fence and call him to come outta there a couple of times." The young woman shrugged, "Oh well. I guess they must live around here somewhere."

Ida checked the fence for breaks and thought no more about the dog that had somehow sneaked in—until one rainy, cold, Comstock afternoon that she will never forget. She'd just sat down to her favorite soaps when the neighbor came knocking on the front door. Somehow the young woman had managed to lock herself out and needed to phone her husband in Carson City.

She stepped into the parlor and glanced curiously around the room. "Oh, Ida! What a lovely home you have."

Then she saw a photograph on the mantel that made her smile brightly. "Why, that's them, the little dog and the man I've seen in your backyard."

Ida smiled indulgently and said, "You're mistaken, dear. That's my husband and his dog. They've been dead going on five years."

The young woman gasped, "Ida! I've seen them as clear as I see you!"

Writers on the Comstock

Walter Van Tilburg Clark, author of *City of Trembling Leaves* and *Oxbow Incident* and editor of *The Journals of Alfred Doten*, is one of many writers who have called the Comstock home. From its earliest days, Virginia City has been a haven for writers. Joseph T. Goodman, Mark Twain, Dan De Quille and Alf Doten are a few of those who've lived and worked on the Comstock.

After World War II, a small writers' colony emerged in Virginia City. Among the writers who discovered the Comstock were Katherine (Katie) Hillyer and Katherine (Katie) Best, freelance magazine writers. Known to their friends as the two Katies, they lived and worked in the Spite House across from the Mackay Mansion. Like Lucius Beebe and Charles Clegg, Hillyer and Best wrote about Virginia City's rich history. Today, it is debated just how accurate some of these authors' historic works were, but one thing is certain: they succeeded in entertaining and interesting those who otherwise might never have visited Virginia City. Hillyer's books include *Mark Twain, Young Reporter in Virginia City* and *Julia Bulette and Other Red Light Ladies: An Altogether Stimulating Treatise on the Madames of the Far West*. Together they wrote *The Amazing Story of Piper's Opera House* and were contributors to the 1953 edition of the *Virginia City Cookbook*.

Katie Hillyer was an avid reader. In the 1950s and early 1960s, there was no library in town, so the bookmobile made regular visits to Virginia City. According to those who remember, Katie Hillyer rushing to or from the bookmobile, arms laden with books, was a regular sight on C Street when the bookmobile was in town. When she died in 1968, you might have thought this would be the end of Katie hurrying to the bookmobile. But you didn't figure on readers and how much they love a good book or writers and how determined they are—and ghosts and how persistent they can be. For many years after her death, Katie Hillyer's ghost was seen numerous times on the C Street boardwalk, rushing to return and old book or select a new one. A sharp-eyed observer might still, on occasion, spot the ghostly bookworm. But that is the problem: unless you recognized her, you might just think she was just another person out on the boardwalk. The books might be a hint, because long gone are the days of the bookmobile.

Lucius Beebe and Charles Clegg

In the early 1950s, bon vivant Lucius Beebe and his partner Charles Clegg came to town. They were enchanted by what they saw in the rustic town full of possibilities. Their first order of business was to buy the *Territorial Enterprise* newspaper and start reprinting it. While they loved trains and stayed in their regally outfitted "Julia Bulette" railcar, which they had named in honor of the unfortunate lady of the evening Julia Bulette, they needed a more permanent residence. They chose the Piper House, which was once owned by Edward Piper, son of Piper's Opera House owner John Piper.

During their time on the Comstock, Beebe and Clegg worked hard to bring awareness of Virginia City to others. Beebe quickly became an activist for the town, and in 1958, the Nevada governor appointed him to serve on the Nevada State Centennial Committee. He also served as the chairman of the Silver Centennial Monument Committee. It was through this committee's efforts that a commemorative stamp recognizing the Comstock Lode was commissioned by the federal government. There is little doubt that Beebe loved VC. He is generally given credit for the resurgence of interest in the town's history and lore. Together, he and Clegg wrote several books on Virginia City's history, including *Legends of the Comstock Lode* and *Virginia and Truckee.*

Even though he died in Hillsborough, California, many years ago, some believe Beebe still resides on the Comstock. His ghost was said to haunt the old Piper Mansion in which he and Clegg lived during their time on the Comstock. Not content to stay in one spot, his apparition has also been seen a number of times in the Silver Terrace Cemetery, staring forlornly off in the distance.

Upstairs at the Virginia City Visitor's Center

Those who work at the Virginia City Visitor's Center share their quarters with a ghost. It's all good though. You see, she was here first. The spry spirit is believed to be either a former owner or a favorite customer of the famous Crystal Bar that occupied the building back in the day.

When Louis Hirshberg opened the Crystal in the Douglass Building on December 1, 1885, he did it up right. Hirshberg served a free roast pig lunch to the enormous crowd of well-wishers. Among them was Comstock journalist Alfred Doten, who took one look around and proclaimed the Crystal Bar to be "the finest saloon in the city."

A few years later, Hirshberg sold out to Con Alhern, who ran the saloon until the 1900s, when he sold it to William S. Marks. Marks had the bar moved from the Douglass Building to its present location in the early 1920s. During the 1940s and 1950s, many a Comstock writer headed to the Crystal

Left: Virginia City Visitor's Center boardwalk sign. *Photo by Bill Oberding.*

Below: Virginia City Visitor's Center. *Photo by Bill Oberding.*

after a hard day at the typewriter. Liquid refreshment and good conversation were always available. A popular spot with locals, the Crystal Bar building remained in the Marks family until the 1990s when it was sold to the Virginia City Convention and Tourism Authority.

Ghostly activity in the building includes the flickering of the ceiling chandelier lights, rearranged papers, misplaced pencils, cold breezes and the strong aroma of cigarette smoke when the building is opened in the mornings. The ghost isn't mischievous as long as things go her way. Two caveats: don't disturb her while she is in the storeroom and don't be surprised if she decides to move things around. One person claims to have heard a disembodied voice angrily order her to "Get out!" as she went into the storeroom. Besides these little quirks, the ghost minds her own business and keeps to herself.

For those who enjoy a good puzzle, there is the Crystal Bar's mystery clock. Just how did this clock manage to keep perfect time no matter how many times its hands were rearranged? No one can say. Certainly, there's a secret to the clock's operation, but it seems to have gone to the grave with the previous owners. Perhaps one of the ghosts will share the secret one day. Perhaps also, the clock will once again keep perfect time. But, as they say, even a broken clock is right twice a day.

The mysterious clock in the Virginia City Visitor's Center. *Photo by Bill Oberding.*

Ghost hunters have spent a lot of time here trying to photograph or record the ghostly smoking lady. On one particular night, our group was not concerned with her. We would leave her to her ethereal cigarettes and go upstairs in our quest for still more ghosts. Can you ever have too many ghosts?

This area was still in the pardon-our-dust stage of remodeling, so we tread carefully. We were told that the upstairs area was at one time a haberdashery and was haunted by a long-ago owner. While we waited for a ghostly appearance, we looked around at the work in progress. Our guide on this night was a woman who worked at the visitor's center and knew her way around Virginia City.

"I've heard that he [the previous owner] could curse up a storm," she told us, and sure enough, there was something X-rated scribbled in Spanish on one of the walls.

"Was he Spanish?" someone in our group asked.

"No, I don't think so," our guide replied.

We smiled to ourselves. Coincidence explains a lot of mysteries. Whoever wrote those words was not in a happy place—and wished the same for *todos* (everyone else). But back to the ghost. Where was he? We called to him, but just as gamblers know that you aren't going have blackjack every time at the tables no matter how much you wish it so, seasoned ghost hunters know that ghosts are never (as in ever *ever*) going to show up on command.

This doesn't mean we can't try. And so we did, again…and again. Although we implored him to do so, the ghostly owner of the haberdashery was a no-show.

CHAPTER 3
THERE'S A GHOST IN MY ROOM

HAUNTED HOTELS

COWBOY GHOST AT THE GOLD HILL

The Gold Hill Hotel was built in 1861 just as the silver rush was getting underway. Originally called the Riesen House, the hotel was purchased by Horace Vesey in 1862 and thus became the Vesey House. It is the oldest continually operating hotel in the state of Nevada. Elegantly appointed with chintz, antique furniture, polished wood and all the charm of yesteryear, the hotel is haunted by a few ghosts besides Rosie and William, who are the most well-known ghosts in residence. One of these is the cowboy ghost who was photographed in the doorway of the great room. The cowboy ghost could be Jabez Spencer, the long-ago victim of a love triangle. Of course, we can't be certain, but as ghost researchers, we attempt to identify the ghosts at haunted locations. This is not always an easy task. We interview witnesses, sift through EVP that has been recorded, evaluate the psychic impressions of others and search old newspapers for clues as to who the resident spirits could be.

Sudden unexpected or violent death can give rise to a haunting. Spencer's death was certainly that. His murder was reported by the *Sacramento Daily Union* on August 27, 1871:

> THE SHOOTING AT GOLD HILL
> The Gold Hill News of August 26th gives these particulars of this affair, mentioned in the Union of that date : At just a quarter-past four o'clock last

evening, town time, shortly after the News went to press, Jabez Spencer was shot and almost instantly killed by James Murray, in front of the Vesey House, on Main street. The circumstances, as near as we can ascertain, are as follows: Jabez Spencer has always been considered an orderly quiet, wellbehaved man, steadily working as an engineer for some years past in the Sunderland and other mills in the vicinity, and lastly, up to the time of his death, in the Mariposa mill. He was forty-one years of age and a native of Illinois. Some four months ago he married a young woman in this town, but we understand that she proved to be of a frivolous, uncertain disposition; at any rate, for reasons best known to themselves, they did not get along well together, disagreeing to such an extent that about three weeks ago he advertised her in the usual form as having left his bed and board without, sufficient cause or provocation, and warning all persons from harbouring or trusting her on his account, as he would pay no debts of her contracting. James Murray is a miner by employment, working latterly in the Segregated Belcher mine, and is also known as a hardworking, steady, peaceable man. He is somewhat younger than his victim, and not noted for getting in any difficulty of the kind before. Spencer had just returned from a short visit to Indiana and rode through to the stand, at the lower end of Gold Hill, on the omnibus. Shortly afterward he walked up the street, stopping to talk at one or two points with acquaintances, and just as he arrived in front of the Vesey Murray came out of the dining-room upon the porch, and seeing each other they each drew a pistol but Murray fired first, and Spencer fell in the street about ten feet from the porch, with his pistol—a Smith & Wesson's seven-shooter—in his hand. He had partially raised it as though to shoot, and fell forward on his face. The fatal bullet had entered his left breast at the shoulder, and ranging downward, pasted through his left breast lodging beneath the lower edge of the right shoulder blade. Blood issued from his mouth and nostrils, and he only breathed a few times after he fell, not living more than a minute. It is alleged that Murray was intimate with Mrs. Spencer, and had threatened to shoot Spencer.

More than a century after Jabez Spencer was felled by a bullet in front of the hotel, a Reno-area photographer who was celebrating his wedding at the Gold Hill Hotel stopped at the door to take a photo of the sunset. He shoots weddings and location portraiture and was amazed to discover the ghostly cowboy in his photo, for he did not see him while shooting. Later, when he showed the photo to his wife, she agreed that the cowboy in his photo looked suspiciously like a ghost.

The photograph has been shown to several photographers and ghost enthusiasts, who have thoroughly examined it. All were struck by the ethereal quality of the original color print. Indeed, it is stunning—but is it ghostly?

After careful analysis, one member of the group stated, "If this is a fake ghost photo, it is the best one I've ever seen." Everyone agreed with that statement.

It should be noted that the photographer is not a ghost photographer, nor does he have any interest in ghost photography. The photo is as much a mystery to him as it is to others who have examined it.

ROSIE AND WILLIAM AT THE GOLD HILL HOTEL

Hotel personnel are used to the ghostly antics of Rosie and William. Both ghosts, they say, are quite friendly and never obtrusive. Most believe William to be the spirit of a long-ago owner, but there is less certainty concerning Rosie's identity. One rumor is that she was an elegant lady who was killed in a carriage accident near the hotel; another story suggests that she may have been a young prostitute who died under mysterious circumstances.

Both spirits make their presence known through strong aromas. It's easy to know when William is nearby; there will be the unmistakable odor of cigar smoke. Rosie prefers the sweet aroma of perfume.

When I attended a ghost lecture at the hotel, the talk turned to Rosie and William. The speaker blithely invited both Rosie and William to join us and continued her talk. Suddenly, the room was filled with the rich, overpowering aroma of flowery perfume. Someone laughed nervously and commented that Rosie was with us. The speaker agreed and greeted the spirit warmly. Then, as quickly as it had permeated the room, the odor of perfume vanished. Apparently Rosie had been acknowledged, and that was all she wanted.

A few weeks later, I happened to have a conversation with the lecturer, who is also a friend. On the night of her lecture, she had occupied Room 4 and her daughter-in-law had taken Room 5.

She related to me:

> *I heard my daughter-in-law get up, open her door and walk up and down the hall several times throughout the night. Just when I'd fall asleep, she'd be up again and stomping down the hall. I know she's into ghosts, so I*

thought she was trying to get a picture of Rosie and William. But there was no need for all the racket she was making, and I intended telling her so first thing in the morning. When I asked her if she got any good pictures [the next morning], *she looked at me like I was crazy.*

"I heard you in the hall last night," I told her. "And you weren't being very quiet about it."

"Wasn't me," she said. "I slept like a log last night."

William usually appears to the cleaning staff as they go about their duties, almost as if he is overseeing them. Rosie prefers making herself known to the hotel's guests. When she's in a playful mood, Rosie will appear to an unsuspecting guest. Don't be alarmed if a beautiful young redhead smiles at you and then vanishes before you have a chance to return the smile; it's only Rosie. If you're interested in staying in the haunted rooms, ask for either Room 4 or Room 5. Sweet dreams!

Talking About Ghosts at the Gold Hill Hotel

What do you expect? Ghosts are going to step out from the darkness and recite some favorite line of poetry? You'd be surprised how many people still think ghosts act on command. They don't. I've lectured on the subject several times at the Gold Hill Hotel, and invariably, someone in the audiences asks why I can't make a ghost appear.

Sometimes, however, we get what we want, and it's not exactly what we expected. Such is the case of a northern California ghost hunting group. One of the burliest of its members rented Rosie's room. Throughout the first day, we made our plans and discussed logistics. He was so eager for Rosie to make an appearance that he could talk of little else. He had his camera and recorder at the ready. If she showed, he was going to capture the evidence.

We had a long weekend ahead of us and turned in close to 3:00 a.m. That's early for ghost-hunting types. Around 5:00 a.m., someone came shrieking down the hall, "She shook my bed! Rosie shook my bed!"

Everyone was up and out of bed. Yes! The big burly ghost hunter, in his blue pajamas, was there in the hallway and scared out of his wits.

"Did she smell of roses?" someone laughed.

He didn't answer. The ghostly Rosie had paid him the visit he wanted, and it had frightened him so much that he exchanged rooms with another group member the very next day.

Miners' Cabin

Every fisherman has a story about the big one that got away, and I know exactly how they feel, especially if they are being truthful and not given to exaggeration. Mine is a story of lost EVP. Over the years, I have presented workshops and classes as part of Truckee Meadows Community College's Paranormal Series. No, you aren't getting credits for ghost hunting, but this series always offers interesting information and speakers.

This particular year, I was working with a group in the miners' cabin at the Gold Hill Hotel. The miners' cabin has been featured on *Ghost Adventures* and, by most reports, is haunted. There were six of us, all female. We tried recording EVP in the far bedroom, and although some ghost hunters insist this is the cabin's hotspot of activity, we got nothing.

In the tiny breakfast nook, I asked participants to sit at the table and turn on their recorders. Because I believe she is gifted psychically, I asked my friend Terri to start asking the questions, like, "Are you here? What is your name?"—the sort of stuff we ghost hunters love to ask spirits.

"Do I have to?" Terri asked.

Knowing what a strong and self-reliant woman Terri is, we all laughed at her mock whine.

She started her questions, and the recorders were catching it all. When we finished the session, I asked participants to play back their recordings. At the very moment Terri asked, "Do I have to?" something very strange was heard. Not only was all of our laughter captured but so was that of deep hearty male laughter. There was no man present in our group. We listened to the recording several more times. Yes, it was a man's laughter. But who was he? Unfortunately, the EVP was lost before it could be examined more thoroughly.

I've talked to several people who claim they could not spend the night in the miners' cabin because it was too eerie. Just as many will tell you that they slept like babies at the cabin. So I decided to see which category I fell into. The cabin was not eerie to me, nor were there any of the purported negative spirits hanging around the night we stayed over. For dinner, we barbecued a couple chicken breasts and prepared a Caesar salad. Napoleon said that an army marches on its stomach, and I agree. If I'm going to hunt ghosts, I may as well do so on a full stomach.

A slice of cheesecake and I was ready to take on the resident bad ghost guys. With cameras and recorders at the ready, we waited…and waited… and waited.

In the end, I slept as well as any baby ever has.

DREAMS AT THE SUGAR LOAF MOTEL

Situated in an area that was known as the "Barbary Coast" and the roughest area in town, the Sugar Loaf Motel is one of Virginia City's newer motels. But that doesn't mean it's not haunted. Like so many other buildings on the Comstock, the motel has its share of ghosts. Some of these ghostly residents are thought to be the ghosts of unfortunate miners who lost their lives during the Yellow Jacket Mine disaster of 1869.

Some guests have reported having their toes gently touched in the middle of the night. Others have awakened to find their bed covers folded and neatly stacked on the floor. A woman who stayed at the Sugar Loaf the summer before this writing said she woke to the sound of someone calling her name. She explained, "It sounded like a child's voice. Don't ask me why, but I got the impression it was a little girl. I was so startled that I jumped up and turned on the lights. That's when she started giggling."

Some of the spirits may be former denizens. Then again, they could simply be pranksters who've decided to check in for a decade or so. Those who don't mind sharing their quarters with this ghostly group should know that Rooms 1 and 3 are their favorite, but there is also the doll room with a Victorian-style doll in a crèche. According to some, the doll itself is haunted. A woman who stayed in the doll room years ago told me that she had pleasant dreams of childhood was sleeping in the room. I didn't dream when I stayed in the room. However, I did have a strange dream when I stayed in another room weeks later. It was a dream of being watched throughout the night, and it kept me tossing and turning.

It seemed that someone was trying to talk to me, and I was trying to ignore the person. His voice became loud and plaintive, and I awoke with a start. I was alone in the room. Could it have been a ghostly miner trying to get my attention as I slept? Or was it that delicious veggie pizza I'd eaten shortly before turning in? It was probably a little of both.

THE SILVER QUEEN

The Silver Queen Hotel has been a favorite with ghost investigators and photographers for a number of years. When Zak Bagans and the cast and crew of *Ghost Adventures* filmed their TV show in Virginia City, they naturally visited the hotel, and just as naturally, they encountered the paranormal here.

Above: The front of the Silver Queen. *Photo by Bill Oberding.*

Right: Silver Queen painting. *Photo by Bill Oberding.*

But let's talk about that painting in the bar with all those coins. The world famous painting of the Silver Dollar Lady, whose dress is composed of 3,261 silver dollars, is probably one of the most photographed sites in all of northern Nevada. Tourists from all over the world have had their photos taken with the unusual painting. In addition to all those silver dollars, the Silver Dollar Lady wears a belt made up of twenty-eight twenty-dollar gold pieces.

Jeri Eaton, a former owner of the Silver Queen Hotel, came up with the idea for the painting back in the 1950s. Ms. Eaton was also the model for said painting. Postcards of Mr. and Mrs. Eaton proudly standing beneath the gaudy masterpiece circulated far and wide. The rumor mill claims that the Eatons' marriage was a rocky one. This apparently was because of a certain little cutie who worked at the local bank. In between cashing checks and taking deposits, she stole Caroll Eaton's heart. There was no need for a divorce. Jeri Eaton died of a gunshot wound one night in her apartment at the Silver Queen.

The death was ruled an accident; she'd been cleaning her shotgun when it discharged, killing her instantly. Psychics who claim to have spoken with the dear departed Jeri Eaton say it was a suicide. Her heart was broken, and there was nothing more she could do. But her widower could do plenty.

Within a few months of Jeri Eaton's death, Carroll Eaton married the bank teller. Before long, he and his new bride were posing beneath the Silver Queen painting. And if that wasn't enough, the verbiage on the postcards was exactly the same as the old—except the new ones claimed that the new Mrs. had posed for the painting. Jerri Eaton was effectively erased from the history of the Silver Queen. But not so fast—you can't easily erase a ghost. And Jeri Eaton is still very much in residence at her hotel. During a recent séance and ghost investigation conducted at the Silver Queen, her presence was noted throughout the evening. She told mediums and psychics that she is not angry. She only wants people to remember her and the part she played in the Silver Queen's history. And that's as it should be.

Tiny, the former owner, is also on the premises. Debbie Bender, owner of the Virginia City Bats in the Belfry Ghost Tour, shared the following. Shortly after Tiny died, two hotel guests came downstairs to check out and complimented the clerk on how friendly the man working up in the hallway had been.

"He told us all about the history of the hotel and even offered us a cookie," they said.

"There's nobody working up there," the clerk assured them.

Left: Old Silver Queen postcard, with Mrs. Jeri Eaton. *Author's collection.*

Right: Old Silver Queen postcard, with Mrs. Ruby Eaton. *Author's collection.*

"Yes, there is," they insisted. "He's a short old man carrying a tin of cookies."

The clerk realized by the description that the ghost of Tiny had spoken with the couple. A diabetic in life, Tiny was not able to enjoy sweet treats. As a ghost, he has no such concerns, hence the tin of cookies.

The hotel was built in 1876 and offers twenty-nine rooms, a quaint wedding chapel and a friendly neighborhood-type bar. I once conducted a ghost conference at the Silver Queen, and I chose to stay in Room 13. At dinner that evening, those of us who were staying at the Silver Queen joked about the ghost. I wasn't too concerned. Being a very sound sleeper, I probably wouldn't even notice a ghost hovering over the bed.

After dinner, we explored the town, and by the time I got back to my room, I was exhausted from climbing Virginia City's notoriously steep hills (take that, San Francisco!). It didn't take long to fall asleep. Around 3:00 a.m., I was awakened by the sounds of a man and a woman arguing. I listened intently as the man's voice grew louder and angrier. The woman's voice was high pitched with fear, as he berated her for being no good and not worth his troubles. She sobbed loudly and begged him not to be so cruel, but he paid little attention to her pitiful pleas for love and understanding. Suddenly came the sound of something being shoved against the wall, and I instinctively reached for the phone. As I did so, I remembered that this was an old hotel without phones or televisions. Now, before you ask, "What about your cellphone," let me tell you that this was in the days before cellphones.

I sat up in bed and listened as he called her a string of vile names. While I tried to decide how best to summon help for her, they started talking softly to each other, and finally all was silent. They had either given up the fight or kissed and made up. Either way, I was too tired to sort it out. Promising myself to report the fight in the morning, I once again drifted off to sleep.

The next morning, the sun shone brightly over Sugar Loaf, waking me to a new day of ghost hunting. But my first order of business: I had to report the abusive man in the next room. After telling the manager about the couple's behavior, I noticed that she was looking at me oddly, almost as if she were trying to determine if I was serious or having fun at her expense.

"You mean to tell me that you've never heard of that couple?" she asked.

My look told her that I hadn't. She smiled at me and explained, "They're ghosts, and they've been fighting like that for over a hundred years."

That night, I tried to record the couple's terrible century-old fight. Unfortunately, both of my attempts to capture the ghostly quarrel failed, with my tape recorder being mysteriously turned off.

Room 11 is said to be haunted by the spirit of a young prostitute, the most heartbreaking of the hotel's resident ghosts. When she found herself pregnant and alone, this long-ago young woman escaped her problem by committing suicide. It was a hasty decision that she regrets. The sound of sobbing is occasionally heard in Room 11, and sightings of the unfortunate young woman are occasionally reported as well. Several people have wakened in the middle of the night to see the young woman's apparition sadly staring at them.

A friend who has lived in Virginia City on and off for several years shared the following experience:

After my divorce, I moved back to Virginia City and took a job as a bartender in one of the saloons. I didn't make a lot of money, so I rented a room in the Molinelli Hotel Building, which houses the Silver Queen, until I could find a larger place.

If I didn't believe in ghosts when I moved in, I certainly did by the time I moved out. I was in the habit of hiding what extra cash I had in a book in one of the dresser drawers. That was okay, until I needed to get it and discovered the money was gone. I turned my room upside down but couldn't find the three twenty-dollar bills that I hidden. No one had gone into the room but me, so I knew it hadn't been stolen; I couldn't figure out what had happened. With no money, I ate crackers for dinner and hoped payday would come fast. Next morning, I woke up, and there was my money right there on top of the dresser.

"Very funny!" I said. Just then, the dresser drawers started to pop open and shut by themselves. I knew then that it was a ghost that moved my money. From then on, I kept my cash with me. My hairbrush, makeup and makeup mirror kept turning up in the strangest places though. I think it was probably the spirit of a child who liked to play little jokes on unsuspecting people.

Clairvoyant/empathic Wayne Pierce, of the group Western Nevada Paranormal, told of his experience at the Silver Queen:

During the investigation, I went upstairs and was standing on the landing looking down at another investigator when I felt eyes on me, like someone was staring intently at me. I turned to see who it was and caught a glimpse of the figure of a man, dressed in 1800 period clothing. He was curious, not malevolent, [and] he just seemed very curious about me and what we were doing. Later that same day I was walking back up the stairs when I felt a breeze on my right side as if someone was walking passed me and trying to greet me as it passed. That wedding chapel at the Silver Queen is always so cold. We didn't spend much time in there, but I felt a presence there as well.

As far as the hotel rooms go, one of our investigators got the feeling the prostitute who supposedly committed suicide in the bathtub was really killed by a doctor somewhere else and placed there in the bathtub. We stayed in Room 11 that night, and Diana woke up sensing someone was in the room with us.

Florence Ballou Edwards and the Silver Dollar Hotel

Let's face it—Virginia City has always attracted colorful people, those who march to their own drummer. Florence Ballou Edwards fit this description. When she moved to Virginia City in 1945, she found a charming town, and she wanted to be a part of it. Edwards bought the Silver Dollar Hotel and spent thousands upgrading it. The hotel was never luxurious, but it was clean. Travelers and those who'd stayed and partied in town until the wee hours of the morning could go upstairs, choose a room and pay up in the morning.

But let's talk ghosts. There's a very good chance that Edwards is the elderly ghost woman who has been spotted in front of the Silver Dollar Hotel on certain nights. She was short and on the hefty side, and this matches the specter's description. Some say there is a little dog with her; others say she is all alone on the boardwalk. Ghost sightings in the old hotel include that of a little boy's ghost and of a teenage girl.

Silver Dollar Hotel. *Photo by Jeff Frey.*

While the Silver Dollar Hotel is no longer renting out rooms, ghostly guests have decided to stay on indefinitely. There are numerous stories of this old hotel's ghostly residents. A woman whose family once worked at the hotel said that years ago, a young couple checked into the hotel after a long day of sightseeing and window-shopping. The trouble started when they couldn't get the ceiling light turned off. Finally, the husband decided that the best course of action would be to unscrew the light bulb from its socket. The light was off, and they happily climbed into bed.

Apparently, the spirit didn't like the darkness. Just as they were drifting off to sleep, the sound of heavy footsteps stomping down the hotel's three flights of stairs woke them. They listened as the heavy-footed person walked out onto the boardwalk.

Curious, they leapt up to see who was making so much noise. There was no one; the street was deserted. They were still trying to figure out what they had heard, when they looked up to see the light bulb in its socket, shining brightly. No matter how many times the man took the light out of its socket, within a few minutes it would be back in and glowing again. Needless to say, they left long before check out time.

Aside from the ghost that doesn't like the darkness, there have been reports of a mysterious crying baby somewhere in the building. The ghostly baby sounds most distressed. That's understandable, considering he or she has probably been crying for more than a century. No one has been able to locate exactly where the crying originates. It seems that the sounds travel from area to area. Just when someone thinks they have located the source of the sound, the crying starts in another area of the building.

CHAPTER 4

HAUNTED COMSTOCK LOCATIONS

FOURTH WARD SCHOOL MUSEUM

No one has been able to determine just why so many old schools are haunted. Nonetheless, I'll hazard a guess: childhood with its carefree days of no responsibilities save homework and tests might have a strong appeal.

There were other schools in Virginia City but none as grand as the Fourth Ward School. The school was built in 1876 so that the children of the Comstock could have a suitable place to learn. With indoor plumbing, toilets, sixteen classrooms and central heating, the Fourth Ward School was spacious enough to accommodate over one thousand students.

It was a modern marvel at its completion, and students eagerly lined up at the sound of the school bell. The *Daily Territorial Enterprise* praised the school in its October 15, 1876 issue, writing, "The pride of Virginia is the new school-house which is going up on the Divide. If it is our pride today, the time is not far distant when it will be our glory as well."

That glory would be one hundred years in coming; by the time the school was completed, the Comstock was already in decline. After graduating its last class of 1936, the school stood empty and forgotten for nearly fifty years. In 1986, the Fourth Ward School Museum was opened to the public. On display were many reminders of a time when the building was alive with the classroom activities of students and teachers.

The four-story structure has been renovated and remains a favorite of history buffs and photographers. Ghost hunters come because of the stories

Fourth Ward School, circa 1950s. *Author's collection.*

of ghostly goings-on within the building and the schoolyard. Several have seen the apparition of a young girl rushing happily down the stairs only to vanish before she reaches the bottom.

Some volunteers at the school have told of the ghostly janitor whose presence is noted by the smell of cigar smoke. Smoking is prohibited in the building, yet the odor of cigar smoke has been noticed in an otherwise unoccupied room upstairs on a number of occasions.

If you happen by the school at night and hear the sound of children's laughter, don't be alarmed. It's only the ghosts of former students trying to catch up on their studies. The specter of a long-dead teacher is sometimes seen hurrying across the schoolyard as if to break up a fight or catch an errant hooky player. Why he is called "Suzette," no one is quite sure. However, during an investigation of the school museum recently, a friend distinctly heard the word "Suzette" whispered in her ear.

There is also the ghostly hitchhiker who stands outside the school on rainy nights hoping to catch a ride with unsuspecting motorists. If you stop to give this apparition a lift, remember that she's only going as far as the Silver Terrace Cemetery.

Above: Fourth Ward School. *Photo by Bill Oberding.*

Left: Fourth Ward School side view. *Photo by Bill Oberding.*

While serving as a docent at the Fourth Ward School Museum years ago, I gave a tour to an elderly gentleman and his wife. It was a cold, blustery day, and the Washoe Zephyrs were fairly shaking the building. As we stood at the bottom of the staircase leading to the third floor, we heard the distinct sound of children running down the stairs. We looked at one another, but no one said a word. A few moments later, we heard the sound of children running back up the stairs.

"It's only the wind," I assured them.

The old man stared at me in disbelief. Then he calmly said, "This building is haunted, and we are leaving!" With that, he grabbed his wife's hand and led her toward the front door. I am still not sure if what we heard that day was the sound of ghostly children or the Washoe Zephyrs rattling the old school. After permitting them for a time, the school/museum was, until recently, closed to ghost conferences and ghost investigations. Thankfully, for us ghost enthusiasts, the Fourth Ward School is again open to us. But one word of caution: always check first.

Virginia City Middle School

You and I may know that ghosts exist. Not everyone would agree with us, just as some may argue that experiences with ghosts have no basis in fact. Very well then, let's see if anyone has an explanation for this next haunted school tale.

Virginia City Middle School looks much like any other school you might drive past anywhere in the country. But unlike those other schools, there's a playful ghost here. According to the person who shared this with me, there is nothing to fear from this specter. The identity of the ghost has yet to be determined or may never be determined, for that matter. Late one afternoon, a janitor was busy vacuuming one of the classrooms when he had an encounter with what he assumed to be a ghost. The students and the teachers had all gone home for the day. He was working alone in the building. The drone of the vacuum cleaner suddenly stopped abruptly. The cord had been pulled from the wall socket. *Things like this just don't happen*, the puzzled man told himself. Before he had time to ponder the cause, the cord began twirling around in the air. That's when he heard a woman's laughter. He looked around the room just in time to see a sparkling on the walls that and moving up toward the ceiling.

A ghost, he told himself. There was no other explanation. Oddly, he wasn't frightened. After all, the ghost was only playing a practical joke on him. As the happy laughter grew louder, the janitor sensed that there was nothing hateful about this spirit. She was merely enjoying his discomfiture.

SILVER STATE NATIONAL PEACE OFFICERS MUSEUM

Housed in the old 1876 Storey County Jail, the Silver State National Peace Officers Museum is dedicated to the history of law enforcement, to the men and women who work for law and order. The museum has an impressive amount of uniforms, badges, old guns, emblems and photos culled from across the country. The bad guys are represented somewhat, and John Dillinger's death mask is even on display.

When it was built in 1876, the jail, with two tiers and ten steel cells, was the largest jail in the state of Nevada. It was used as Storey County's jail from 1877 until 1987. Imagine how many criminals spent time here. Among them was the infamous Joe Conforte, one-time owner of the Mustang Ranch Brothel. Apparently some of these former inmates have come back to haunt

Former Storey County Jail, where the Peace Officers Museum is housed. *Library of Congress.*

the museum. Misplaced display items, unexplained noises and a shadowy figure who roams near the cells have made some of those who volunteer here question whether the museum is haunted. I have heard bizarre claims of people having been scratched by unseen forces while recording EVP in some of the cells. Having never been scratched in all my years of ghost investigating, I am always skeptical of such claims—unless there happen to be some ghostly cats in the area. Cats scratch, but ghosts—no.

The Delta Saloon and Casino

On a cold snowy night in December 1887, light came to Virginia City with the lighting of the Old Magnolia Saloon. It was cold on the Comstock. Snow was piled six inches deep on the sidewalks. As darkness overtook the city that night, electric lights shone for the first time on the Comstock. The Delta Saloon (Old Magnolia Saloon) became the first business in town to use the electric light in its establishment.

The "suicide table." *Photo by Bill Oberding.*

Delta Saloon boardwalk sign. *Photo by Bill Oberding.*

Of special interest to ghost hunters is the ghostly man in black who is said to wander the saloon at all hours. This could be the ghostly "Black Jake," original owner of the faro table, known as the "suicide table." They say that Black Jake lost $70,000 at the table one night. Unable to cope with his losses, Jake shot and killed himself. He wouldn't be the last person to lose heavily at the table, nor would he be the last person to take his life as a result of losing it all.

In 1890, the new owner of the table lost $86,000 dollars while playing faro at the table. Like Black Jake, he killed himself when faced with such financial ruin. As others who played at the table turned up dead, it gained such a bad reputation that no one would play at it.

Wisely, the owners removed the table from the playing floor. This didn't stop actor Jack Palance and the Columbia Studios TV film crew of *Ripley's Believe It or Not.* They came to Virginia City on May 21, 1984, and filmed a segment of Palance dealing cards on the suicide table while he told of its dark history. The Delta Saloon is proud of this event, and a photo display near the suicide table proclaims, "It was a day the Delta Saloon will never forget."

But what of the Black Jake, did he make an appearance during filming? Apparently, he was camera shy. But some who've spent time in the Delta Saloon claim to have seen the ghostly man in black walk through the walls as easily as one might call for a refill. Perhaps Black Jake has returned and is hoping to end his long losing streak. There's something about that suicide table that draws him back, again and again.

The Death of General Jacob Van Bokkelen

Provost General Jacob Van Bokkelen was the original owner of the land that St. Mary's Art Center stands upon. It was here that his popular drinking spot, Van Bokkelen's Beer Gardens, was located. And then, according to an old Virginia City legend, his pet monkey started playing with Van Bokkelen's nitroglycerin. The result was a disastrous explosion that killed Van Bokkelen, the monkey and several other Virginia City residents. Some say there was no monkey. Monkey or not, there is another mystery to this story. Was Van Bokkelen killed in the explosion—or was he murdered by angry residents?

The *Sacramento Daily Union* of July 1, 1873, reported on the explosion:

Terrible Explosion in Virginia City, Nev.
Ten Persons Killed and Many Wounded. Several Buildings Blown Up and Burned.
Virginia, Nev., June 30th. There has been a terrible explosion of giant powder in Root's building. The building was burned. The two upper stories of the bank building were also burned out. Ten persons were killed. The tire is out.

Additional Particulars—Names of the Killed and Wounded. Virginia. City, June 30ᵗʰ. Last night, at 10:45 o'clock, a terrible explosion of nitroglycerine and giant powder occurred in this city near the corner of Taylor and Li streets, killing ten persons and wounding many others. A large number of bodies are missing, and probably buried beneath the debris. The explosion, it is supposed, was caused by six cans of nitroglycerine exploding without any apparent cause, and the concussion of that exploding 150 pounds of giant powder, all of which was stored in or beneath the room of General Van Bokkelen, who was agent in this city for giant powder. The following buildings were shattered and partly thrown to the ground: Bank of California and buildings to the rear of it, Kennedy & Mallon's grocery store, Douglass' building, used in the upper apartment as a lodging-house, Daly's saloon and Armory Hall…The number of persons now known to be killed is ten, among whom is Major-General Jacob L. Van Bokkelen, J.P. Smith, hardware merchant, William Davis, clerk, with J.P. Smith; Benj. Maudell, dry goods merchant; Chas. H. Knox of San Francisco, John Devine, Mrs. Emily O'Connor, formerly of the International Hotel in this city, Ed. Dean and daughter, 8 years of age, of Gold Hill. The body of General Van Bokkelen was found in a corner of what was his room, his features so bruised and charred as to be hardly recognizable. J.P. Smith and former clerk were found in Taylor Street, between B and C streets, about fifty feet from the room occupied by them. Both bodies were covered with the debris of the fallen walls and were not gotten out till this morning. Some of the firemen saw Knox last night, and spoke to him. He asked for water, and said: "Boys, it's no use. You can't save me." His body, with the exception of the head, was entirely covered by the fallen timbers and brick. John Devine was killed by an iron door which was hurled a distance of about 100 feet. A large number of workmen are now engaged in removing the dirt and timbers from the bodies of the seven known to be beneath them, and are working with almost superhuman efforts. The buildings in all directions are shattered, and many near escapes were bad. Samuel Doak and Charles Biggies were thrown down from their room in the Douglass building to Daly's Exchange, and were got out with difficulty, both being slightly injured. D.L. Blanchard was thrown from his room to another, several yards distant, yet escaped with slight injury. Great excitement was caused last night by the screaming of women on top of the Douglas [sic] building, which was at one time in flames. They were finally rescued by Captain Frank Osbiston, assisted by the firemen. Another explosion took place this morning at 10:30 in the rear of Kennedy & Mallon's store, but no person was injured. 10:45 a.m.—The body of Charles H. Knox has just been taken from the ruins. It is horribly charred and mangled. The city is all excitement; business is suspended and all the schools are dismissed. The streets are crowded with men, women and children. Ropes are drawn across the streets, as the walls of the buildings are considered dangerous. The vault of the Bank of California is cracked in several places, and their business has been removed to Driscoll & Tritle's banking house. It is now understood that there will not be any celebration of the Fourth of July, and that the money collected for that purpose will be expended in burying the unfortunate dead, and the remainder distributed among the different fire companies of this city. The city will go into mourning, and all the flags are now at half-mast. Joseph Sharon, Dan Lyons, Charles Haugender and Senator Hobart, who were reported killed, are all safe. It is now ascertained that Van Bokkelen had stored beneath his room six cans of nitroglycerine, 150 pounds of giant powder and 200 pounds of black blasting powder.

This could account for some of the paranormal activity that takes place at the Washoe Club and other buildings in the area of the explosion.

St. Mary's Art Center

The Daughters of Charity (also known as the Sisters of Charity) came to Virginia City in 1864 to open a hospital and a school. With the death of Jacob Van Bokkelen twelve years later, his beer garden was closed and his land was available. This is when John Mackay's wife, Louise, acquired the land and donated it for the new hospital that was built in 1876. The building stands to this day. It is an art center in which artists from around the world come for residencies to display and teach their techniques and to work. This might not have been possible if not for the efforts of Father Paul Meinecke of St. Mary's in the Mountains. In the late 1960s and 1970s, the building was going to be dismantled for its bricks. Working with others, Father Meinecke was able to save the building, converting it to the art center.

There are at least two ghosts believed to haunt the building. The White Nun is the most well known and the most often seen. Over the years, both residents and tourists have seen the apparition staring forlornly from one of the building's third-story windows late at night. Indeed, she is occasionally spotted in daylight as well. My son Fred and his wife, Peg, and I drove up to

St. Mary Louise Hospital, circa 1890s. *Author's collection.*

tour the building one day several years ago. As we pulled into the driveway, there were no cars parked in front, and I wondered if it was even open.

"There's someone here. I just saw somebody staring out that window," Fred said, pointing toward the center window where the ghostly nun is most often seen. We knocked on the door several times, but there was no answer, and we were about to leave when the caretaker came from around the back of the property. We asked about the people staying in the building, and he looked at us strangely. "No one is here but me, and I haven't been in the building since early this morning."

Why does the White Nun haunt the building? Fate sealed her doom one night long ago when a terrible fire broke out in the hospital. People were mad with fear, scurrying for safety. As the flames leapt higher, the brave young nun tried desperately to help her patients escape the danger. She managed to save many of them before being overcome by smoke and perishing in the fire.

Dressed in white from head to toe, the lonely nun's ghost is usually seen in Room 11, the former chapel. She walks the halls of St. Mary's Art Center calmly checking on the welfare of her patients. Those who have felt her presence say she is a kindly spirit. A former student at the art center opened the door of her room and saw the phantom nun sitting on her bed. She smiled sadly and then vanished. Later that evening, the ghost returned to pull the covers up and carefully tuck the student in. People have told of meeting a heavyset woman who smells of violets in the building's kitchen. Some say they have awakened from a deep sleep only to see a ghostly figure trying to take their temperature. Others mention the sound of a hospital gurney screeching its way down the hall late at night.

Over the years, several ghost investigations and conferences have been held at St. Mary's Art Center. During one of the investigations, a woman spotted the specter of an elderly man in a wheelchair in the corner of the art room. He seemed confused, like he didn't really know where he was. The darkroom on the ground floor was particularly ominous to some investigators, who felt a negative male presence there.

The standard EVP words were collected on the stairs that lead to the attic when an investigator taped a shrill woman's voice shouting, "Get out!"

Ghost Hunt at St. Mary's

Several years ago, I was presenting a retreat at St. Mary's. The second day of the event was a gorgeous November day on the Comstock. Participants were out exploring, visiting the C Street shops and saloons and partaking of the many activities Virginia City offers. My grandson Justin and I were staying in the little room at the front of building. While everyone was out, I was catching up on my reading and Justin was taking photos. But did he have to be so noisy? I had had enough when he came stomping down the staircase.

I stepped out of the room to confront him, saying, "Justin, please quit making so much noise!"

No one was on the stairs.

"Justin?" I called.

No answer. I was alone in the building. I opened the front door and saw Justin sitting at the picnic table on the front lawn. "How long have you been out here?" I asked.

"Awhile now. Why?" he replied

"I thought I heard you on the stairs."

"Must have been a ghost," he laughed. Must have been.

That evening, the group was hit with EVP fever. Armed with recorders, we were at the side door and attempting communication with those on the other side. "Can you hear us?" someone asked.

"Yes," came the reply. Excitement was in the air. We had all heard the voice clearly. Talk about "Class A"—this had to be something spectacular going on.

"We're here to investigate, and we mean you no harm. What is your name?" we asked the voice.

The door handle rattled. Was this a friendly spirit?

"Will you make the door handle move again?" we asked.

It did—and some investigators stepped a few paces from the door.

The handle rattled again. "I am locked out," the voice said.

Locked out! But a ghost can walk through walls.

"What do you mean?"

"I'm the caretaker, and I'm locked out. Will you please open the door?"

So much for Class A EVP that night.

Séances at St. Mary's

While I don't necessarily believe that much evidence is gathered during a séance, I do see the séance as a tool that may help to open communication with the afterlife. Others might disagree entirely, and that is fine with me. I have conducted three séances in St. Mary's, each with a different group of people and each with different results.

The first séance was held in 2001 and was conducted in the large artist room. The séance consisted of a small but vocal group of participants, with names and visions being called out frequently. One of the most remarkable things about this were some of the disturbing impressions that sitters received. These included people, particularly children, being mistreated and buried on the property and a nun having been sexually assaulted here as well. Although the séance was held on a warm October night, the sense of a heavy rain and thunderstorm pervaded the séance circle.

One spring a decade later, I took part in a fundraising event at St. Mary's by presenting a second séance upstairs. Nothing negative and dark, mind you, but an attempt to communicate with those ghosts who might be in residence. We sat in a circle, and ghost investigator Paula Burris lent an air of elegance to the séance by playing her flute.

A large curtain was placed at the window, and the wind whipped it continually throughout the evening. Many of us felt that several spirits walked into and out of the room that night. It was far different than the first séance I had ever been a part of at St. Mary's.

The third séance was humorous. An impromptu circle of chairs was formed in the basement, the door closed and we began. Little did we know that one would-be participant had had a bit too much to drink at dinner. She knocked on the door again and again, until finally we let her in. There was one vacant chair. She rushed to it and sat, but her aim was off, thanks to the alcohol. She missed the seat and went right down to the floor. The séance was concluded in howls of laughter. Hopefully the spirits had a sense of humor. Regardless, they would have to wait another night.

Clock Watchers at St. Mary's Art Center

Paula Burris is a busy woman. As a pit boss at one of the local hotel/casinos, a full-time student at Truckee Meadows Community College, a web designer, a photographer and a ghost investigator, when does Paula have time to sleep? While I pondered this, the sparkly eyed grandmother was set to tell me about her encounter with a clock at St. Mary's Art Center.

Angela Coleman, former caretaker at St. Mary's, was doing a special Halloween weekend event with Debbie Bender (Bats in the Belfry Virginia City Ghost Walk). Paula was asked to come up and help out. Never one to turn down an investigation at St. Mary's Art Center, she readily agreed. Paula would be leading tours of the building. She started a tour off at 10:30 p.m. and was in the attic at five minutes to midnight. After being up in the attic for about forty-five minutes, she noticed that the clock's hands were moving too fast.

It was definitely not an electrical surge, as this was a cheap, battery-operated clock, so Paula checked the batteries. Just to be certain, she replaced them. With Paula and her group watching, the clock's hands kept speeding along. They tried the K-2 meters and got very high readings from the clock.

On a hunch, Paula said, "Making this clock run faster isn't going to make the sun come up any sooner."

The clock's hands slowed and began to move in real time.

This phenomena with the speeding clock happened three years in a row, and some of it was filmed. But not all of it—at one point, Paula had her hand in motion, ready to film, when suddenly the clock's hands started moving normally again. No one can explain it.

A speeding clock isn't always a bad thing. Wouldn't it be great to have a ghost activate the clock at work like this?

PIPER'S OPERA HOUSE

The movie *Somewhere in Time* is said to be one of the most rented movies of all time. It might never have been written if writer/screenwriter Richard Matheson hadn't visited Virginia City and Piper's Opera House. While at Piper's, Matheson saw a photograph of Maude Adams, an early actress. Her beauty so inspired him that he got the idea for the cult favorite fantasy, and the rest, as they say, is showbiz history. And showbiz history is a good place to begin the story of Piper's Opera House.

From its beginning, Piper's Opera House was destined to be the Comstock's cultural center. When fire destroyed his opera house, John Piper rebuilt on the corner of Union and B Streets. Then came the morning of October 26, 1875, when the Great Fire raged across Virginia City. Once again, flames swept through Piper's Opera House, demolishing it in a matter of minutes, but John Piper would not be beaten. An astute businessman, he rebuilt an even grander building in the same location, and the opera house stands to this day.

On opening night, January 28, 1878, snow was nearly four inches deep on the Comstock, but it didn't deter Virginia City residents from celebrating the opening of the new Piper's Opera House. The elegant building was hailed by the *Territorial Enterprise*, which called it "the best of its size on the Pacific Coast." The new opera house was the place to see and be seen in Virginia City. In an age before television, radio and movies, Comstock residents gathered at Piper's to enjoy performances by some of the world's most famous lecturers and entertainers. The list of luminaries who have either performed or attended performances at Piper's includes President Ulysses S. Grant, Edwin Booth, Henry Ward Beecher, Maude Adams, Lily Langtry and Mark Twain.

Most old opera house buildings such as Piper's are long gone, the victims of runaway progress, a new-is-better attitude and an accommodating wrecking ball. Thankfully, this is not the case with Piper's Opera House. The people of the Comstock treasure the building; it represents the last vestige of times past. Here is our opportunity to see how those who came before us entertained themselves. They did so without benefit of central heating, air conditioning, microphones, surround sound and computer-generated lighting effects. Theaters and opera houses have long been known as the favored places of ghosts. Perhaps this is because of the array of strong emotions that are played out within their walls; plays are rife with emotions such as anger, revenge, lust, hatred and love. As these are

Piper's Opera House today. *Photo by Bill Oberding.*

continually portrayed in the theater, some part of the emotion may linger over time, drawing spirits like a magnet. There is also the possibility that showbiz is just too difficult to give up; once dead, an actor or actress may seek the familiar comfort of a stage.

When the spirits of long-ago performers tread the boards in Piper's Opera House, they do so before ghostly audiences who are also said to haunt the building. People who enjoyed attending theater performances in life may see no reason to curtail that enjoyment. The sound of audience laughter and soft applause has been heard emanating from Piper's long after the lights have gone down and the building is empty. In addition to the performers and the audiences, the ghost of John Piper is said to linger in the opera house. Piper was an elegant dresser who enjoyed the pleasures of a fine cigar. It seems to be a habit he has carried beyond the grave. Cigar smoke has been noticed in unoccupied parts of the building for many years. Sightings of Piper have also been reported, especially during a production's opening night performance.

Ghost Hunt at Piper's Opera House

I was taking part in an investigation at Piper's when one of the participants noticed a ghostly woman float across the balcony. This apparition is believed to be the wife of a long-ago Comstock millionaire. She wears a bottle green velvet dress and is usually seen in the balcony or one of the private boxes. As investigators quietly checked their meter readings, a man's voice said, "Good idea!"

Perhaps it was John Piper himself letting us know that he approved of our investigation. Even though the woman's apparition had been seen, meter readings in the balcony on this particular night were low, indicating only nominal activity. The stage seemed to be the "hot spot" of activity. Meters spiked when a sensitive in the group softly whispered that there were several spirits near him on the stage.

Sleep Over at Piper's

Let's dispense with the rumors. Houdini did not appear here at Piper's Opera House any more than George Clooney appeared in my living room. It's a technicality; during the 1940s, the opera house was a movie theater, and Houdini appeared via newsreel. And the Houdini legend went around. So this means that technically George Clooney did appear—oh, never mind.

The old opera house is a favorite with ghost hunters because everyone usually gets something: EVP, photographic anomalies and, yes, moving orbs on video. Love them or hate them, orbs do show up in photographs at Piper's. A few years ago, a local television anchor took a crew up to Piper's for a Halloween story. They got a tad bit more than they expected. When they got back to the station and listened to the interviews, they discovered some strange voices on the audio portion. The sound engineers could not find any explanation for the voices.

They say that John Piper himself roams the building. How do they know it's the ghostly Mr. Piper? No smoking is permitted in the old building, but Piper ignores the rules and continues puffing on his cigar. Other sightings include ghostly ladies and gents who have been spotted in the boxes. Several years ago, an investigator was tapped on the shoulder while photographing in one of the boxes. That's not as bad as it can get. The ghost who causes the most sensation is the one that pinches the bottoms of women in the dressing room.

Imagine that it's opening night, you've got a case of jitters and your friends have stopped by to wish you "break a leg"—and then some ghost pinches you on the behind. Pretty scary, but's this is exactly what happened to an actress friend of mine. In fact, she's been pinched several times at Pipers. She laughs it off. After all, how do you slap a ghost's face?

Over the years, numerous ghost investigations have taken place within Piper's Opera House. Most ghost hunters agree the building is haunted. Most theaters and opera houses are. Think of the famous people and the egos that tread these boards. In ghost lore, a healthy ego is one reason for ghost activity. A few years ago, a group was conducting an overnight ghost hunt of Pipers. I was invited to take part, but something told me not to go. Mostly my husband, who had invited my in-laws for dinner, but I'd also like to say that intuition also told me to stay away.

As it turned out, a local newspaper columnist was included in the group. In those days, ghost hunters were naïve enough to believe that all journalists were as enthused about afterlife antics as they themselves were. The columnist got her story, and it was interesting all right. It was a humorous take on the event, detailing how nothing unearthly showed up and how loud ghost hunters can snore. Those who put on the overnight event were not impressed with the article. I got a very good laugh out of it and a nice sigh of relief. Thank goodness I wasn't there to add to that cacophony the reporter wrote about.

Piper's Opera House Investigations by Western Nevada Paranormal

Wayne Pierce, clairvoyant/empathic of Western Nevada Paranormal, shared the following on his group's investigations of Piper's:

Most ghost groups don't get to go in the attic, but someone asked the tour guide if we could go up there and she allowed our group access. As we climbed the narrow stairs, I sensed something not right. I got ten to fifteen feet from the door and something told me, "Don't go any further."

Diana and another investigator went to one of the theater boxes in the far right corner, and they sat in the chairs. Diana jumped up and said, "I feel like I'm on fire!" Later, she asked the tour guide about the chair and was told that the chairs had been in a fire.

On our next investigation of Piper's, we were joined by a group from San Diego. We got a lot of activity and evidence on the stage. I would class it as residual. Backstage there is the energy of two people, a man and a woman. It was so strong I could feel the energy bouncing off me. In the left box stage left, we tried to get EVP, but something kept telling me to go on stage. For some reason, I was directed to go to the center of the stage and stand there. I don't know why, but the next thing I know I heard (in spirit) a shattering like wood snapping. I felt like something hit me in the back of my neck. I went to my knees.

As I composed myself, I heard the words, "I'm sorry. I didn't mean to. I didn't know she was pregnant. I don't know what to do. I don't know where to go." The voice was very despondent. I felt someone sitting there, and I believe the voice was that of someone who hanged himself in Piper's. Later, I was told that someone actually did hang himself in Pipers.

MACKAY MANSION

The "Mackay Mansion" is a name that might shock John Mackay. He didn't live in the house very long, and according to a longtime Virginia City friend who wrote the following letter, Mackay's wife never lived there at all:

Here are the facts. John & Marie Mackay & family lived in a house at the corner of Howard & Taylor. John built a home in San Francisco which the family moved into around 1870 after a trip to Europe. The VC house was burned down during the Great Fire in 1875. Mackay moved into the Mackay Mansion after Marie and the family moved to San Francisco. Marie and the family did visit VC from San Francisco but NEVER resided or even stayed in the Mackay Mansion. The mansion was Mackay's office & a place to live when he & partner James Fair were working & taking care of business.

But Johnny Depp did stay here while he was in Virginia City filming *Dead Man*. During this time he is said to have encountered the ghost of little girl in the mansion. This little ghost has appeared to others countless times.

A Mackay Mansion tale that intrigued me was that of the punctual ghost that appeared at the safe in the mansion every afternoon at 3:00 p.m. sharp. Well, we would just see about that. My friend and I armed ourselves with cameras and recorders and made our way up Geiger Grade early enough to be on time for the appearance. We met a tour guide, and the three of

Mackay Mansion with Sugar Loaf in the left background. *Photo by Bill Oberding*

us waited…and waited…and waited. She assured us that he (meaning the ghost, of course) always comes through the door and enters the safe at the same time every day. But on this day, he was a no show. Where he was, there was no telling.

The mansion was originally built by George Hearst as the office of the Gould and Curry Mining Company. When the Great Fire of 1875 fire swept through town, destroying hundreds of buildings in its wake, Comstock millionaire John Mackay found himself without a home and took up residence in this building. Mackay was a generous man who treasured the simple things in life. His wife, however, preferred the elegance of Europe to the wild and rowdy Virginia City. While she traveled and eventually settled in Paris with their children, Mackay lived alone. By all reports, he was quite happy during the time he spent in his mansion.

Area brides consider the mansion romantic and often choose its gazebo for their weddings and receptions. The ghosts seem to enjoy the festivities. A few years ago, a guest at one of the weddings told me that she actually saw the specter of an elderly woman smile broadly just as the groom kissed the bride.

There are said to be at least three ghosts in the mansion or its vicinity, though no one is really certain who they all are. For years, people have told of seeing an elderly lady dressed in period clothing sitting in the downstairs parlor. There is also the ghostly child upstairs who insists on jumping up and down on the bed and leaving toys strewn about.

The apparition of an old army colonel has been seen in the kitchen area many times. He is believed to be a previous owner who died here. For whatever reason, he has decided to stay on in the mansion indefinitely. The ghost of a Chinese man has been seen in the area surrounding the mansion's carriage house and gazebo. He is believed to be the ghost of a man who died while attempting to warn others about a terrible fire that was raging nearby.

Séance at the Mackay Mansion

A snowy night was predicted for the Comstock, and it was welcome, what with the drought northern Nevada has been enduring for several years now. Those of us who didn't live in Virginia City were headed up Geiger Grade for a séance at the Mackay Mansion. Snow and fog covered the roadway. Such a night for a séance! After dinner at the Del Rio, it was off to the Mackay Mansion.

Walking into the Mackay Mansion, you can't help but notice that a somber mood permeates the old building. Ghost hunters will tell you that it's haunted. Some will even say that the Mackay Mansion is one of the most actively haunted spots in Virginia City, and some of the spirits here are not necessarily the friendly sort. Tonight the dining room was no warmer than the outdoors. The heaters were not on, and there was no fire in the fireplace. *Just like the old days*, we comforted ourselves with the thought as we lit the tall candles at either end of the table and proceeded to open the circle by calling only for positive spirits to come. Holding séances in Virginia City is a time-honored tradition among ghost enthusiasts or, as we call ourselves, paranormal people. Hopefully, we would be visited by some of those who had come before us.

The first person we called was Louise Mackay who may or may not have lived here in Mackay Mansion but a short while. If Louise heard us in the beyond, she gave no indication. One of the mediums in attendance saw a woman who was apparently stuck in the mirror. We asked that this ghost come into the circle and speak with us. One sitter had several impressions of a little girl who was present. Could she be the same little girl ghost that Johnny Depp encountered?

"Give us some sign that you hear us," we implored.

There was no response. Then the spirit of a man with a health issue who stayed upstairs was sensed. A sitter with long, red hair sensed a man with a respiratory problem come into the room. She could hear him wheezing as he moved nearer to her. A real shock came when she jumped up, saying, "Something just pulled my hair!"

We asked that one of the spirits present herself, and two of us heard someone say, "Never!"

We clearly heard heavy footfalls overhead, knocking throughout the room and a strange scratching sound. We got the names "Annabelle," "Samuel" and "Lanson." As the evening wore on, the temperature in the dining room was unbearable. We attempted to close the séance circle, but something did not want us to end the séance. A second attempt was made, and the circle was closed.

St. Mary's in the Mountains

In the predawn hours of October 26, 1875, a kerosene lamp was knocked over during a drunken mêlée in Crazy Kate Shea's A Street boardinghouse. Wind-driven flames quickly spread out from the building and raced down the hill. Before it could be contained, the fire swept through the north end of Virginia City, leaving ashes and rubble in its wake. Thousands of residents were left homeless, and just as many buildings were destroyed, including the original St. Mary's in the Mountains church. It was an especially cruel blow to Father Patrick Manogue, who, a few years earlier, had lost his brother James in a terrible train accident near the Norcross Mine. The unfortunate James's legs had been severed when he fell from the train. Beyond hope, he was brought to Saint Mary's, where he died a short while later.

A Virginia City story has Comstock millionaire John Mackay promising the townspeople that he'd rebuild the church if they would allow all firefighting efforts to be directed toward saving his mines instead of their church, and so they let their church burn. Mackay was a generous man of his word. He kept his promise, and St. Mary's in the Mountain was rebuilt. The church's silver bell that was recovered from the ashes was placed in the new church in 1877.

Some believe that the kindly spirit of Father Manogue is still in residence at the church. Father Manogue was an Irish immigrant who came to the Comstock in 1862. A strong-willed man who wasn't afraid to fight for what

Virginia City Middle School with St. Mary's Church and St. Paul's Episcopal Church in the background. *Photo by Jeff Frey.*

he believed in, he was much beloved and respected by the community. By the time he left Virginia City in the early 1880s, his congregation numbered well into the thousands.

The good father became a bishop and later died in Sacramento on February 27, 1882. While some folks believe that Bishop Manogue has returned to Virginia City and oversees St. Mary's in the Mountains to this very day, others insist that it is really Father Meinecke who is the resident spirit in the beautiful old church. He walked with the use of a cane and had a distinctive footfall. This is why some say he is the church's resident ghost. Father Meinecke died of a self-inflicted gunshot wound in his apartment at the church on May 16, 1974.

There is also the phantom hunchback who has been seen around the area of the church. When he realizes that someone has seen him, the specter turns and flees in terror before vanishing into thin air. If you visit, please be aware that the church is still in use.

St. Paul's Episcopal Church

In the early days of Virginia City, St. Paul's Episcopal Church boasted one of the finest pipe organs in the state of Nevada. Members of the congregation were very proud of the instrument, which had 1,100 pipes, the tallest of which was sixteen feet. Apparently a ghostly old woman is so proud of the church that she never wants to leave.

The elderly woman's apparition has been seen in the church many times over the years. No one can say for sure who she is, but those who've seen her say that she seems to be very angry about something. A man who'd done roofing at the church said that he and some of his co-workers knew the church was haunted. Apparently, no one liked going up in the attic because of the eerie feeling there. Was it the angry old woman? Though they'd felt uncomfortable in the attic, no one saw her apparition.

A friend who is affiliated with the church told me that most of the congregants know it is haunted, although few will discuss it. They don't believe there is a mean old woman haunting their church but rather a positive spirit who just happened by. St. Paul's Episcopal Church is located on F Street near St. Mary's in the Mountains Church. Although the congregation is small, the church is still in use.

The Chollar Mansion

The Chollar Mansion was built in the early 1860s, adjacent to the Chollar mineshaft, and served as the residence of the superintendent, Billy Chollar. After a lengthy lawsuit that was rumored to have cost the opposing parties more than $1 million, the Chollar Mining Company and the Potosi Mining Company agreed to merge their holdings and become the Chollar-Potosi Mining Company. In 1870, it became apparent that the sides of the shaft could no longer support the building, and it was moved north a quarter mile. Today, the Chollar Mansion is a delightful bed-and-breakfast situated behind the Fourth Ward School. The mansion is home to a few ghosts whose identities have been lost or forgotten with time.

A ghostly gentleman seems to enjoy walking up and down the mansion's stairs—and that's some exercise. You see, there are more than forty stairs in the house. When not climbing the stairs, the ghost likes to spend time at the bookcase on the second-floor landing. In life, he was probably a voracious reader. He's been spotted taking books out of the bookcase, carefully examining them and then angrily slamming them back into the bookcase. Perhaps he doesn't approve of the reading material. Then again, he could be looking for something that he hid in a book long ago.

The painting that hangs in the Chollar Mansion dining room was discovered in the attic during renovations. There are those who believe that this is indeed Billy Chollar. Whoever he is, the gentleman in the painting does match certain eyewitness descriptions of the mansion's gentleman ghost, who has been described as a darkly handsome, mustachioed man in his mid-forties. Other accounts describe the spirit's as much older, silver-haired and not so handsome.

The ghostly gent may have been a loner who preferred the company of his books to that of his fellow man. It's a trait he seems to have carried beyond the grave. He likes to keep to himself and abhors noisy crowds. Whenever a special event brings a large number of visitors to town, the ghost seeks solace on the third floor or the storage room. Quiet, please!

Little Missy Duncan died of a childhood disease in the mansion long ago. Apparently Missy hasn't gone far. Her apparition is seen more often than any other Chollar ghost. The barefoot Missy's hair is in ringlets, and she usually appears in a long, white linen dress. This ghostly child is a snoop who loves to forage through guests' luggage while they sleep. One guest told of waking in the night to see a little girl pulling things from her suitcase. When she demanded to know just what the child was doing, the woman was shocked as the ghostly Missy turned and walked through the wall. Another woman told of seeing the little ghost hover over her bed.

Missy startled a young couple awake one night when she suddenly appeared in their room. "How did you get in this room?" the husband demanded. Without waiting for an answer, he jumped up to escort the little girl out. When he attempted to open the door, he discovered that it was still locked and bolted. Missy smiled sweetly before dissolving into thin air.

The noisy ghost occasionally moves things around. When a guest complained to the owners that their redecorating kept him awake all night they were mystified. Early risers who rarely stayed up late, they soon realized it was only one of the mansion's ghosts having a little fun.

During the Comstock's heyday, thousands of dollars worth of silver and gold bullion were kept in the 164-square-foot vault. Temperature variations in the vault are quite noticeable. This could be because the vault is underground, but it could also be because at least four ghosts are said to reside within the vault. Thought to be the spirits of miners who perished in a mining accident, the ghosts enjoyed being mischievous in the kitchen. Noisily stomping around, turning water off and on and clanging pots and pans seemed to be among their favorite pastimes. Over the years, they've quieted down somewhat. This no doubt pleases the ghostly gent who covets peace and quiet. The Chollar Mansion is a private residence.

Television Show Notes and Ghosts

Who doesn't like being on television? Tell the truth now. The plethora of reality shows belies any argument that most people would rather watch TV than appear on TV. These shows also give credence to Andy Warhol's statement about everyone having his or her fifteen minutes of fame. So lights, camera, action! Reality TV loves Virginia City. This is especially true of shows (local and national) that focus on ghosts and hauntings.

Antiques Roadshow

What do you think I said when a friend e-mailed me to ask if I would be interested in doing an appearance on *Antiques Roadshow*? I said, "Yes!" of course.

She explained that the show was going to be in Reno and wanted to get up to Virginia City and do some filming. I had no antiques for valuing, and God knows I don't consider myself an antique, but oh yes, I was interested. The schedule was set. And after a day at the beauty salon, I was ready for my close-up and set to tell some ghost stories.

I met Lara Spencer and the crew at Piper's Opera House in preparation for filming at the cemetery. Lara Spencer is one of those lucky people who is more beautiful in person. Besides that, she's nice. She asked a few questions about Virginia City, and we were off.

It had rained late that afternoon, turning the sky that lovely reddish gold hue it can take on after a good thunderstorm. The cameramen remarked how unusual the sky was and hoped they could capture it. They did—and none too soon. Darkness quickly fell across Virginia City as we drove toward Silver Terrace.

We would not be stopping at the usual front entrance. We would be traversing to the oldest section in the very back. Tonight it seemed almost gloomy, lit only by a crescent moon that hung over Sugar Loaf. It was perfect weather to be in the cemetery. And then voila! Before anyone could think about the dead who reposed here or the ghosts that might roam here, presto, the battery packs and lights went on. Old headstones were shown and explained. The ghosts who reside here were mentioned but did not make an appearance. And then it was done. But ghosts are like that. You really can't count on them. They will appear when you least expect it, in their own good time. Besides, this show was about antiques, and the area ghosts were not given a starring role.

Ghost Adventures

Ghost Adventures is the number-one ghost hunting show on television today. Recently, the cast underwent a change with the departure of Nick Groff and the addition of Jay Wasley and Billy Tolley. I think Zak, Nick and Aaron will continue being successful no matter what project they are involved with. Only time will tell how Nick's absence is going to affect the show. I met Zak Bagans, Nick Groff and Aaron Goodwin when they were just starting out. They were enthusiastic and excited to chase ghosts. The same on camera as off, they were never too busy or self-absorbed to sign an autograph or chat with a fan, and their fans adore them for this.

I was fortunate enough to have been invited to take part in their first two live ghost hunts and to appear on their Goldfield episode and a Virginia City episode as well. After talking with Zak, I was set to take part in the Virginia City show. On the scheduled day of filming, I had my hair done and then drove up Geiger Grade. Now I was ready for my close-up, Mr. DeMille.

I parked down on D Street and walked up the hill toward the old Washoe Club. Patting my freshly done do, I was glad that we would be filming inside. But no, plans had changed. Zak wanted an outdoor shot. Did I mention that the wind was blowing fifteen or more miles per hour? Never mind, we got into the van and off we went on the lookout for a suitable location, over to Gold Hill and back and then up into the hills high above Virginia City. Here Zak found the perfect filming site. By this time, the wind was really whipping up. It didn't take long for my new hairdo to be transformed into something I hadn't anticipated. However, my hair color looked enchanting. So much for money spent at the salon that day. But there I was, talking about ghosts on camera with Zak.

The author with Zak Bagans, Nick Groff and Aaron Goodwin of *Ghost Adventures* in front of the Washoe Club. *Author's collection.*

In the Basement at the Territorial Enterprise Museum

Not every filmmaker who comes to town has a television show and a production company. Some are amateurs hoping to make it big with a great documentary of Virginia City and its ghosts. When a friend of a friend came to shoot a documentary on Mark Twain and the ghosts of Virginia City, I agreed to help. And so one warm fall night, we converged into the basement of the Territorial Museum, where Twain's desk was. Hanging nearby was a nicely done portrait of the humorist/writer. Whether the humorist actually worked at this location is much debated, but this hasn't stopped ghost hunters from bringing in their regalia and setting up a hunt.

The apparition most people see is not Mark Twain at all but rather a man in a dark tailcoat who stands halfway up the stairs, shouting orders to those in the basement. Some say it is Dan De Quille (William Wright) or long-dead editor Joseph Goodman attempting to get his cadre of slowpoke ghosts to meet an impending deadline.

While I don't necessarily ascribe to the theory that orbs are spirits, I have seen some phenomenal video that was shot in the basement in total darkness. On this night, the new filmmaker was very careful to have everyone involved sign his release form. That's standard. And he was learning. After collecting the releases, he set up all the cameras and mics. So far so good—until one person walked in front of camera B so many times that it seemed almost a designed play. Do you see me now?

The filmmaker took the offender upstairs to explain the protocol. The person smiled slyly. "Oh yeah?" he said. "Well, I didn't really want to be in your film anyway."

"Then why sign a release?" the befuddled new filmmaker asked.

"That? I signed a phony name to your release, so…"

Needless to say, the entire shoot was ruined because without signed releases from those who appear on camera, the footage will most likely never be used. But hopefully the filmmaker learned a valuable lesson.

Haunted Bars and Restaurants

Businesses come and go, especially in Virginia City. The ghosts remain, and so do the buildings, though the businesses contained within may change. So it is that the Sargent Major's bar is no more. Today, it is the Silver Dollar Saloon.

The sun was setting, and the wind was stirring up a dust cloud far out beyond Sugar Loaf. This was the wind described by Mark Twain all those years ago, the winds he called the Washoe Zephyrs. Anything that wasn't nailed down went flying. But only for a while—by the time darkness fell across the Comstock, all was calm.

My husband and I were lucky to find two seats at the bar. It was Saturday night, and the place was busy. Over the raucous noise particular to bars everywhere, we ordered, and I explained why we were there. I had made arrangements beforehand to see the so-called haunted spot here in the saloon.

We were taken to the basement, where we examined bricks that came out of the kiln somewhere around 1859. I'd been told that this is where a ghostly woman is sometimes spotted. We had been told that she was believed to be a long-ago prostitute who was hiding from someone. Another prostitute ghost—this town has a number of them. The life of a prostitute on the

Comstock was one of loneliness, danger and squalor. Oftentimes a woman saw no way out and took her own life.

But the person who had led us to this spot in the basement knew nothing about the specter. No point in asking questions, so we took our photos and headed back upstairs where word had traveled fast; more ghost hunters were afoot.

The entertainer decided to have some fun with us. "Walk like a ghost," he sang, his fingers deftly sweeping across his keyboard. Now think about that if you will. Just how does a ghost walk?

"Ghosts don't walk, they float," someone shouted to him over the noise.

If we are to believe conventional wisdom, this is true of the ethereal among us. But the amps were at full level. He couldn't have heard the retort even if he wanted to.

"Walk like a ghost," he sang. *Are there no more lyrics to his hastily devised song?* I wondered. Probably not, but it was all in good fun. The very moment a ghost hunter, researcher, enthusiast starts taking herself or himself too seriously, all is lost—especially here in Virginia City.

Knights of Pythias Building

Ghost hunters have long thought that the Knights of Pythias building is haunted, and ghost investigations seem to bear this idea out. Several years ago the Mandarin Garden Chinese restaurant was housed upstairs here. The restaurant was a family favorite. Whenever we were in Virginia City, this is where we invariably ate. So it was that my daughter-in-law and I stopped in one day. Laughing and talking, we were halfway up the stairs when we noticed a man open the front door and start climbing the stairs behind us.

At the top of the stairs, we turned to look at the stranger who'd followed us up the long staircase. Imagine our surprise when we discovered that we were alone on the landing. The man had been there just a few feet behind us. We'd seen him come in the door and heard his footsteps on the stairs. There was no place he could have disappeared to, no other doors and no other place he could have gone—in this world anyway. We put the experience down to either a resident spirit or a curious ghost who'd followed us into the building.

This was at a time when digital cameras were still brand-new gadgets. My daughter-in-law had just bought herself a digital camera and was ready to show it off. She stopped and quickly snapped a few photos. Though she didn't get a photo of the ghostly man on the stairs, she did manage to get an orb. Once seated, and our selection made, we asked about ghosts in the building. Our server smiled and said, "Maybe."

Café del Rio

So you're here and you're hungry—you've found the perfect place. Brian and Ardi Shaw have worked hard to make their Café del Rio a Virginia City favorite. They serve enchiladas done in a special way, and let's not even talk about the Wednesday night Gospel Fried Chicken or the crème brûlée.

The Café del Rio is housed in the old Werrin building, which dates back to 1873, when John Werrin, a Cornish grocer, operated a grocery store on the ground floor and a boardinghouse on the second floor. Of all the lodgers who stayed here at the Werrin House, it seems one may still be in residence. A local medium visited the building several years ago and believes the spirit's name is Margaret. In her honor, the Shaws have named the newly remodeled banquet room upstairs Margaret's Room.

On the night before Halloween, just before the banquet room was ready for service, my husband and I visited the Café del Rio with friends. Halloween is the State of Nevada's birthday, so there is always a lot of celebration. The atmosphere was one of anticipation as patrons and employees, decked out in costumes, awaited festivities on the Comstock. After dinner we asked, and Ardi, dressed as a witch, kindly agreed to take us upstairs.

The original brick wall remains, as does the C Street view. The track lights may be twenty-first century, but they add a nice yesteryear glow. Margaret must be very happy with the new banquet room. We went out onto the balcony and looked out toward Sugar Loaf. Below us was C Street with cars and nowadays noises, but out toward the east, a full moon was rising, giving us a brief glimpse of how it might have been when John Werrin rented out these rooms. And speaking of Mr. Werrin, long before Brian and Ardi Shaw opened the Café del Rio, a friend of mine thought of buying the building as a second home. People who had lived there thought the ghost of an elderly man haunted the place. They told her that every morning just before sun up, the aroma of coffee and frying bacon wafted through the building even though no one was cooking. The ghost of Mr. Werrin immediately comes to mind. If it is him, he probably enjoys the kitchen of the Café del Rio very much.

Grandma's Fudge

Who doesn't love fudge and candy apples? No one I know, and this place produces some of the tastiest chocolate candy around. Shoppers can stop and watch a big batch of fudge and other chocolate concoctions being made right there in front of the store at a large window. No one should be surprised that there is a ghost or two on the premises.

A former owner told me that once in a while heavy fudge pans have toppled off the refrigerator while she was busy in her office. There is no earthly way the pans could have fallen without someone's assistance.

Recently, I stopped by for some divinity (diet be damned) and to ask current owner Jim Ward about the ghosts. While he hasn't had any ghostly experiences, his employees say the place is haunted. Then, too, there was that day his wife was busy in a backroom of the shop when she heard him calling her name. She came to the front to see what he wanted—but when she asked why he had called to her, she discovered that it wasn't Jim who had been calling her.

Grandma's Fudge boardwalk sign. *Photo by Bill Oberding.*

Jim Ward, owner of Grandma's Fudge. *Photo by Bill Oberding.*

Most likely it was one of the shop's ghosts having some fun at the owners' expense. Was it the ghostly little girl who's been heard laughing and crying, or was it the spirit of a long-dead schoolteacher who's been spotted here on occasion? Take your pick. Whoever the spirit was, she probably has a sweet tooth, and I can't say that I blame her for choosing this place to haunt.

COMSTOCK ANTIQUES

Located in the Douglass Building, the same building that houses the Washoe Club, Comstock Antiques sells an array of eclectic items. Vintage clothing, posters, china, handmade jewelry—you name it, and you might just find it here.

And while you're at it, you just might encounter a ghost or two. My friend Richard St. Clair told of an experience he had one day while working in the shop: "I was alone in the store and working in the back when I happened to notice movement. I looked and saw the shadowy figure of a woman moving really fast. She had her hair up in a bun and looked like someone from the 1800s."

You'd be hard pressed to find a building in town that isn't haunted, and everyone knows it. So the next time I was in town, I asked the other employees about ghosts. "Oh yes," they readily agreed, "there are ghosts here." But do they want to be disturbed by them? Never! In fact, one woman told the ghosts not to ever show themselves or bother her, and so far, that seems to have worked.

Home Sweet Haunted Home

The shops and the cemetery aren't the only haunted locations in Virginia City. Many (probably most) of the older houses here also have a ghost in residence. Most of the time a ghost will be a compatible roommate, but not always.

While speaking at a conference in Virginia City several years ago, I met a woman whose family was being besieged by a ghost who liked to play with her crystal knick-knacks late at night. She didn't know what to do and was at her wit's end. More than once, she was awakened by the tinkling of bells. After investigating the strange noise, she would discover that her collection had been rearranged. The trouble was that the playful spirit sometimes misplaced the knick-knacks altogether.

The more upset she became at her collection being mishandled, the more she found herself and her children the victims of a cold draft that no amount of heat could dispel. In fact, the ghost seemed to favor a place near the wood-burning stove. Whenever the family sat near the stove, they invariably found themselves in the path of an icy draft. A group of us investigated her little D Street house and kindly asked the ghosts to skedaddle, pretty please. She also burned sage and asked the ghost to vacate. Eventually, it came down to a choice: live with the ghost or move. She moved from the house.

A midwestern couple relocated to Virginia City, intrigued by its Wild West aura and its ghostly goings-on. Little did they know, their unfurnished rental included a ghost. Just as they were drifting off to sleep one night, they suddenly found themselves wide awake when a photograph came crashing off the wall. The wife checked the wall to see the nail still firmly embedded, and the cord on the back of the picture was still intact. It wasn't

Ghost investigation, old school. Note the old cameras and equipment and the ghost mist to the right. *Photo by Peggy Oberding.*

an earthquake. The house was built about the same time that Rutherford B. Hayes was residing in the White House, so this couldn't be attributed to the house settling.

They accepted the Virginia City obvious: their house was haunted. So they called in ghost hunting friends for advice. Burn sage and say prayers were the suggestions. They did so, but the ghost wasn't impressed. Things continued to fall from the walls, and night after night, heavy thuds were heard overhead. The couple lost sleep. More sage and more prayers were advised, but still, the ghost wasn't budging. He or she had been here a lot longer and wasn't going anywhere.

They thought about looking for another rental. Surely there was a small house here that wasn't haunted. But what if there wasn't? And just suppose this ornery ghost followed them to their next abode, then what? Their Virginia City dream was slowly falling apart. You can either be happy on the Hill or not. This couple decided that they could not. So they packed up and headed back to the Midwest.

CHAPTER 5

THE WASHOE MUSEUM

THE WASHOE CLUB: BEGINNINGS

The Washoe Museum housed in the Washoe Club is easily one of the most famous locations with ghost hunters. Ghost hunts and conferences regularly take place here. Easily the most elegant attraction has to be the spiral staircase that served as the entrance to the Washoe Club from the Crystal Bar at one time. In 1876, the unique staircase was added during remodeling of the second floor. It is believed to be one of only two known such spiral staircases to exist in the United States. The other staircase was built in 1878 and is located in the Loretto Chapel in Santa Fe, New Mexico. Neither staircase has a supporting beam. And although that of Loretto Chapel is larger, it is believed that both were built by the same mysterious carpenter. The staircase is the perfect place for the ghostly Lena to make an appearance.

Known as the most haunted location on the Comstock, the Washoe Club began with a simple idea. The Washoe Club would be a place for Comstock millionaires to rub shoulders with others of their same financial standing. It would be fabulous, as befitting its members' standing in the community. The *Territorial Enterprise* of February 20, 1875, reported the following on the Washoe Club:

> *We understand that the club will either purchase or erect a suitable building in which to fit up their rooms, and it is their intention to have everything in grand style. There will be a fine library and all the leading newspapers*

Above: Washoe Club. *Photo by Bill Oberding.*

Left: Washoe Club sidewalk sign. *Photo by Bill Oberding.*

of the United States will be kept; also, the stock reports and all also in the way of news will be brought to the rooms of the club. There will be a billiard-room, lunch room and all else that is to be found in the rooms of any first-class club of the kind. The number of members is limited to 200. This club will supply a want long felt in the city, and is calculated to do a vast amount of good in a great variety of ways. The names of those who are taking the lead in organization of the club are a sufficient guaranty [sic] that it will prove a grand success in every respect.

Two months later, in April 1875, a suitable building was found. The Reynolds Building on B Street would be the location of the chi-chi Washoe Club. Then, as today, the goings-on of the rich and famous captured the public's interest. Then, as today, there was a news source eager to tell the public everything. The April 22, 1875 issue of the *Territorial Enterprise* shared these details:

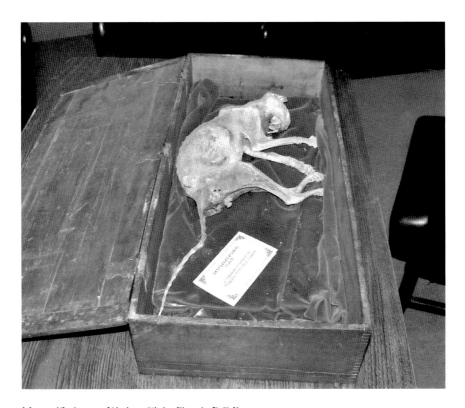

Mummified cat at Washoe Club. *Photo by Jeff Frey.*

The double hall was at once taken out and the stairs, which were in front, were removed to the rear. As at present arranged, the ascent is easily made and the hall commodious. The lower floor of the building is still occupied by Mr. Thompson, the architect, upon one side, and by Mr. Hereford, the mill and mining superintendent, upon the other. To the north of the hall, and next to the eastern wall, is the wine-room—14×17 feet—which will be fitted up with an elegant sideboard, etc. Between this and the front parlor is the card-room—14×14—which is to be elegantly furnished, but in which no games for money will be allowed to be played. Passing through the folding doors to the front, you enter one of the double parlors, which occupy the whole front of the building, and are connected by sliding doors of ample dimensions. The first parlor is 19×24, the second 24×27 feet. To the west of the one last mentioned is the billiard-room, 24×31 feet, which is to contain two tables, of elegant pattern and most approved make. Either of these rooms is accessible from the hall and communicate by means of sliding doors. The old windows are to be removed and replaced by two panes of French plate glass. The carpets and furniture are to be of the most elegant styles and make and of superior quality. The grates and mantles are of the purest marble, and when completed, the Washoe Club will have a place where they may recline at ease and sojourn in comfort. It is the intention of the Club to erect a building upon the western portion of their lot, and facing "A" Street, which will be fitted up in elegance and used as a really first-class lodging house with restaurant attached. When completed, the Club may justly feel proud of their conveniently arranged, elegantly fitted up and comfortable rooms.

Virginia City truly was a city of the haves and have-nots. Imagine how the men who worked long, grueling hours in the mines felt when they read the news of the ostentatious Washoe Club. Perhaps there wasn't a lot of other news going on, because the details kept coming. More news of the Washoe Club followed in the June 4 issue of the *Territorial Enterprise*:

The situation is most desirable being on "B" Street, between Taylor and Union, and a few doors north of the Court House. The front is adorned with a balcony, from which the magnificent scenery to the east of the city is visible. This outlook is unsurpassed by any in the land. The eye ranges over the busy part of the city, the hills to the east, the Sugarloaf, the Valley of the Carson, the Como Range, and on till its reach is lost in the distance. Upon the background of the picture, the Twenty-Six Mile Desert, 65 miles away,

Looking through the doorway of the Washoe Club. *Photo by Bill Oberding.*

appears as a brown spot, and the Humboldts, 150 miles distant, raise their bold broad brows, snow-covered, till they seem to mix with heaven's blue arch and fade away to the sky. The faint outline of the Forty-Mile Desert, so terrible in early days as the abode of dusty death, is just caught as it sinks, like the dip of ocean water, behind the intervening ranges. The approaches to the rooms are easy and elegant. The lower hall is ample and well lighted. Toward the western end the stairway rises very gradually, taking 32 steps to gain the elevation of the second story. The hall above is also ample, well lighted, and affords easy access to each of the rooms. The stairs and upper hall are elegantly carpeted with body Brussels. The front part of the second story is occupied by the parlor and reading-room.

The parlor is 27×24 feet. The carpet is of body Brussels of elegant make and extra quality. The same pattern extends through the reading and billiard-rooms. All the carpets were selected for the Club by Mr. Rogers, President of the Union Club of San Francisco, who has certainly displayed superior taste in the selections made.

The mantle [sic] is of the finest Italian marble and adorned with beautiful bronze statuettes, the one in the center bearing an elegant clock, those at either hand representing Shakespeare and Tasso, respectively. Above the mantle is placed an elegant and costly French plate glass mirror. The walls are finished with China glaze and ornamented with distinguished works of art, and conspicuous among them were noticeable the two storm scenes by French, the one representing "Broad River Falls," North Carolina, the other "Haymaking," and each having a storm done to nature for a background. These elegant paintings were purchased at the recent art sale in this city. The windows are of fine plate glass and the furniture upholstered, the covering blending and harmonizing beautifully with the carpet.

The general description above given to the parlor applies equally well to the reading room. This room is 19×24 feet, and is to the left of the parlor. Here are to be found all the latest papers and periodicals for perusal. The paintings on the walls are also very fine and include a "Summer Scene in Orange County, New York" and Zang's famous "Winter Scene."

The chandeliers, both here in the parlor, are of elegant pattern, beautifully gilt and the finest ever brought to Virginia City. Large sliding doors connect this room with the parlor, as the two are fitted up en suite.

The billiard-room is carpeted with the same body Brussels as the parlor and reading-room. It contains two elegant tables manufactured by Strahle & Co. with Delaney's patent wire and rubber cushions and slate beds. Here everything is of the same style of elegance as prevails throughout the entire establishment. Even patent counters are introduced, thus doing away with the necessity of stretching wires across the room. This room is to the right as the upper hall is gained and communicates by sliding doors with the parlor.

The wine and card-rooms are to the left of the upper hall and communicate with the reading-room. These are richly and tastefully furnished and contain everything which can contribute to the comfort and enjoyment of those who frequent them. These rooms are respectively 14×17 and 14×14 feet. The card-room is back of the library, and the wine and lunch-room in the rear of the card-room. The sideboard in the latter is of black walnut, elegantly and elaborately carved. Next to it is a sink of the same material and made to correspond therewith. The carpets in both rooms are of the same pattern and differ in figure only from those in the other rooms. The chandeliers in these rooms are most elegant and covered with steel plate, which is polished like silver.

The store-room is on the lower floor, where all the supplies are kept. The whole is under the immediate supervision of the Assistant Secretary, W.C. Brown. All supplies are charged to him. When anything is needed by the bar-tender upstairs, it is charged to the sideboard. Members partaking thereof or engaging in billiards, hand to the bar-tender a card prepared for the purpose, which is filled out with the name, article and amount. No money is used by the members. Their accounts are all kept and charged up and kept with their monthly dues.

And then, just before dawn on October 26, 1875, a kerosene lamp got knocked over during a fight at Crazy Kate Shea's A Street boardinghouse. The Great Fire swept through Virginia City, destroying everything in its path. The Reynolds Building that housed the elaborate Washoe Club crumbled in the flames.

It was now necessary to find a new location for the Washoe Club, and that is where we find the Washoe Club today. As you look around the empty upstairs area today, envision the building as it was described in the *Territorial Enterprise* of September 3, 1876. And while you're at it, ask yourself if you believe the long-held rumor that it has a secret passageway that enabled prostitutes to sneak into and out of the Washoe Club. And if you believe that, ask yourself if the lovely and ghostly Lena might have been one of the ladies who visited the posh Washoe Club and if any of those millionaires might stick around in ghost form. I bet they do!

Left: Stairs where activity occurs Washoe Club. *Photo by Bill Oberding.*

Below: View from the ballroom of the Washoe Club of St. Mary's Church with St. Paul's Episcopal Church in background. *Photo by Bill Oberding.*

The Washoe Club rooms in the Douglas block are now nearly completed and more elegant than those on "B" Street which were consumed by the great conflagration of last October. They are also more conveniently located, being within easy access of both "C" and "B" Streets, and in the busiest part of the city. They comprise, in all, eight apartments, all of which are fitted up with elegance and taste. They are reached by a flight of stairs from "C" Street and also by steps from "B."

The reading-room fronts on C Street and is lighted by four large windows of French plate glass. The apartment is 30×22 feet. The floor is covered by an Axminster carpet of the thickest and finest make and most elegant pattern. In the center of the room is a 4 by 12 table of black walnut inlaid with laurel, on which are all the papers and periodicals usually read on the coast. The room is abundantly provided with upholstered furniture in the shape of easy chairs, sofas, lounges and the like. On each side are placed $800 mirrors of French plate glass in frames and mountings manufactured expressly for the porch of the building in front. In the evening the apartment is brilliantly lighted by two chandeliers of polished steel. The reading-room is separated by folding doors from the billiard-parlor.

The billiard-parlor is in size its exact counterpart, so that when both rooms are thrown together an area of 22×60 feet is gained. It is lighted from the rear by day and by silvered chandeliers by night. The carpet of this parlor is of same pattern as that of the reading room. It contains two Strahle tables of the very best make and latest improvements, the beds being of slate and the legs, etc., beautifully carved. Wilton carpets with mitred corners surround the tables. The markers are peculiar institutions and were manufactured expressly for the Washoes at a cost of $100 each. They consist of small black walnut stands, from the sides of which rise arms branching out about a yard. These are connected by wires on which are strung ivory buttons. The counting is done with the fingers and thus the unsightly and inconvenient wires across the room are avoided. A stationary washstand occupies one corner and the parlor is amply provided with furniture. This room communicates with the hall and main entrance and also with the wine-room.

The wine-room is connected with the billiard parlor by means of a broad, arched doorway, richly and heavily draped with crimson curtains, which are drawn aside during the occupancy of the rooms. This room contains an elegant sideboard amply stocked with the very best beverages and cigars which can be procured and a lunch table bountifully supplied with delicacies and substantials. It is richly carpeted with body Brussels.

This room is adjoined on the west by the card-room, which is carpeted like the wine-room and furnished with all the appliances which belong to such places.

These apartments and the reading-room and billiard-parlor are daily thronged with the members of the Club and their guests. A stock-reporting telegraph gives regular quotations from the market, and its registerings are narrowly watched while points are given and exchanged among the members.

Between the wine-room and the hall are the reception and storerooms. The former is conveniently arranged for the use of members and visitors. It is provided with hat-racks, and at one side are arranged a number of boxes for the reception, in stormy and bad weather, of mudshoes, etc. The store-room is provided with facilities for storing in proper order the supplies for the wine-room and such other things as are necessarily kept on hand for the convenience of the Club.

Across the hall and reaching to the front of the building are two private card-rooms, which are also being prepared with the proper furniture and necessary accommodations for the members in this line.

Taken all together, the rooms are more convenient, better arranged and more elegantly and luxuriously fitted up than were the rooms which were occupied by the Club previous to the fire.

The end came in 1897. By that time, the mines had played out. The Rush to Washoe was history, and the millionaires had either left town or died. There wasn't enough money being brought in through memberships to keep the Washoe Club afloat. The September 9, 1897 issue of the *Territorial Enterprise* told the story: "The Washoe Club is no more. The closing of the Washoe Club marks an era in the history of Nevada, as did its opening."

During the 1930s, the upper floors of the building were converted to apartments. According to some, this was the not a place of the highest class. I believe that much of the ghostly activity at the Washoe Club comes from this era rather than an earlier time when the mines were flourishing. Some deaths and suicides took place in the Washoe during this time period. That's not to say that death and suicide automatically give rise to haunting activity, but we do know that one ghost who has been reported is that of a man who hanged himself here in the 1990s.

Right: Washoe Club tour guide and member of Empathic Paranormal Richard St. Clair unlocks the door to go upstairs at the Washoe. *Photo by author.*

Below: The author upstairs at the Washoe Club. *Photo by Richard St. Clair.*

Séance with the *Ghost Adventures* Team

The *Ghost Adventures* team (Zak Bagans, Nick Groff and Aaron Goodwin) hadn't yet hit the big time, paranormally speaking, in 2007. They were three young guys who'd done an award-winning documentary at the Goldfield Hotel and were now out promoting it and looking for ghosts. Virginia City was their destination of choice, particularly upstairs in the ballroom at the Washoe Club, where all the ghostly activity was said to happen. Besides, this is where Nick caught sight of a full-body apparition and Aaron filmed it. Now they had returned to Virginia City to do their first paranormal conference. They called it a Live Ghost Hunt Weekend.

I was invited to help host their weekend event, along with Dave Schrader ("Darkness Dave") and other researchers/investigators. In addition to investigations, a séance was planned. Granted, there is nothing scientific about a séance. But let's not forget that ghost hunting, research and investigation is experimentation. We should never be afraid to experiment or to combine different methods. Besides, this wasn't to be an ordinary séance, in which ghosts are summoned, questioned and sent back to wherever it is they'd came from.

This would be a séance that incorporated state-of-the-art technology. In this case, cameras and computers would be recording the séance for playback later, to see if we could capture instrumental transcommunication (ITC). None of us were experts in ITC. We had a rudimentary understanding of the principles and knew that researchers had been achieving some outstanding results with ITC, so we had no reason to doubt that we might capture a ghost face on the monitor during our séance.

We had seen presentations by Mark Macy (who is an expert),

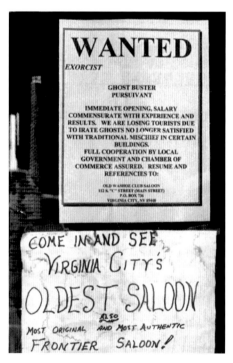

Notice posted in front of Washoe Club regarding ghosts circa 2000. *Photo by Bill Oberding*

The Washoe stairs during the day. *Photo by author.*

as well as Tom and Lisa Butler's images of people who had come across through ITC. It sounded like such an interesting concept. But let me just say here and now that we received nothing with this experiment. Win some, lose some. Experimentation is an important part of ghost investigation and research. We tried. But the séance—now that was a different story.

There were about twenty-five of us sitting on the floor in the area where several people were said to have died. We joined hands and opened the séance circle by asking for only positive energy to come to us. Only those with the highest and best intentions were invited to cross over from their world to ours. Nothing…

Nick Groff was holding my left hand as he and Dave Schrader began some challenging. "Show us what you got!" they said. As usually happens, it wasn't the challenger who got the first hit. A woman who was sitting across from us had her head tapped by an unseen force. Startled, she screamed.

This really fired up Nick and Dave, who said something like, "You can pick on girls, huh. Well, pick on us." I silently hoped the ghost would have a good sense of direction when, and if, it chose to accommodate them. Nick was ready to say something more when suddenly his hand turned ice cold and he was trembling. I turned to look at him, and he certainly didn't look very well. He said he was feeling nauseated. And yes, the taunts stopped. Some of us either saw or felt a presence walk behind us. Whatever had come into the séance circle was obviously angry and didn't like what Nick and Dave were saying. No one should seriously believe that all ghosts are friendly. They are not. And this, if nothing more, was clear evidence of that.

We decided that now might be a good time to close the circle and end the séance. But before we could do that, a woman started crying as a little girl's spirit came through her, telling us of an abusive life she'd lived in Virginia City. Her story was heart-rending. When she had finished, we closed the séance circle and began investigating the ballroom.

GHOSTLY CHILD

Perhaps there is more than one ghostly child here at the Washoe Club. A little girl's ghost has been spotted numerous times on the second floor. Those who've seen her describe this ghost as a frightened little girl in a tattered, old-fashioned white dress. She is painfully shy and vanishes the moment anyone notices her. Some believe that she is the ghost of a young girl who died in a runaway horse accident nearby more than a century ago. On October 20, 1864, a runaway buggy came racing down C Street. One of the passengers was a young girl, who fell out of the buggy, breaking her neck. The unfortunate child's death was noted in that day's edition of the *Territorial Enterprise*. This may well be the little ghost upstairs.

The ghostly Peter is a young boy who stays in a closet on the third floor. Some psychics feel that he was

Richard St. Clair shows where he saw ghosts. *Photo by author.*

the victim of parental abuse. My friend Richard St. Clair, a tour guide at the Washoe, collected EVP of Peter. Other investigators have caught glimpses of him on the second floor.

Who Is in the Crypt?

The crypt is a controversial subject among ghost hunters and historians. Voicing one's beliefs on the crypt may not be as socially foolish as discussing politics and religion, but it's close. For those not familiar, the crypt is the back area of the Washoe Club. Presently it is in the back of a paranormal museum that features a lot of ghost hunting paraphernalia used by Zak Bagans and the *Ghost Adventures* team and others. Fans of *Ghost Adventures* are in for a treat here. But there is more: there are the ghosts. And there is the story, and that leads us to the controversy.

Why is an area that was used for storage in a saloon referred to as the "crypt"? It derives from a tale that's agreed to be fact by many. Bodies were

Jason Ball enters the crypt. *Photo courtesy of Jeff Frey.*

The author at the door of the crypt. *Photo by Terri Hall-Peltier.*

once stored in this area, not a large number of bodies but some. In the winter months when the ground was frozen solid, no one could dig a decent grave. This left the problem of what to do with the bodies. The story goes that they were taken to the back of the Washoe Club and held in the cold area until the ground thawed. Seems logical to me, but the question does arise: why not use the undertakers' facilities?

That would depend on how many bodies there were and how large of an area the undertaker had. Those who accept the story have been calling the area the crypt for a while now and saying that this building wasn't the only one in town to have occasionally stored bodies. Those who don't accept the story—well, the arguments continue. In the meantime, this is in back of the area where the paranormal museum is located, and it is haunted by a couple ghosts.

One of them has been known to lock women in the ladies' bathroom. This locked-door phenomenon is not exclusive to the Washoe Club; it has been reported at various locations throughout the country. Why ghosts do this is anybody's guess.

Richard St. Clair, who is a tour guide at the Washoe Club, and I were in the crypt recently when he told me the following incident: "I was in the crypt with a psychic. I was sitting, and she was standing. This place is cold, but the space next to me felt even colder. The psychic looked at me and said, 'There is someone sitting next to you. It's a man named Hank, and he wants you to know that he really likes you and the work you are doing here.'"

What the Tour Guide Saw and Heard

My friend Richard St. Clair is a tour guide at the Washoe Club who has had numerous experiences while leading tours and investigating there. He wrote the following the night he and his group Empathic Paranormal investigated the Washoe Club:

It has been established early on by a few psychics that Lena has taken a strong liking to me. I'm a tour guide at the Washoe Club, and she likes it when I'm there. On this particular evening there were three investigators; Jud, myself and Cimarron who is a psychic. Cimarron picked up that Lena was present and she wanted to come into the room so she could be near me.

Cimarron told her it was ok to come in. She entered the room and came right up to me, and she started to stroke the top of my head. I could actually feel her doing it. I said to the rest of the investigators in the room to get a picture of me right away. There is a picture we think is Lena lifting off of the top of my head. Just as this was happening, Cimarron got that Lena had a message for me. And she had a surprise for me. And that was the end of the haunting. At that point, we really didn't know what that meant. We went through the rest of the night doing our investigation, [and] at around 6:00 a.m. we decided to call it quits and start closing down the investigation. Cimarron, Jud and I went into the second floor apt (above the crypt) to take some extension cables down. As I walked into the room, there standing in one of the doorways was Lena. She was showing herself to me. I gasped and turned to ask the Jud and Cimarron if they were seeing this. As I did so, she took off backwards out of the doorway and back

Washoe tour guide and member of Empathic Paranormal Richard St. Clair demonstrates where he saw a ghost. *Photo by author.*

down the hallway. Neither Jud nor Cimarron saw her, but they did hear the swooshing sound and the energy in the hallway. It was like boards were being cracked as she went down the hallway. We think what I saw was the surprise that Lena conveyed earlier in the investigation that she had for me.

Richard believes that the third floor is the location of more negative spirits. He told of seeing a crawling man, moving on all fours like an animal, and of having another spirit rush right through him as it made its way to the bannister railing.

Show me a ghost hunter, researcher or psychic/medium who doesn't want validation—that is, proof that the evidence we collect (EVP and photographs) and the feelings we sense have some basis in fact. This is why the following that Richard told me really made me wonder: "I was on the third floor and I sensed the little boy around me. He said, 'Get back to work, Rich.'"

In the following story, a ghost also tells investigators to "Get to work!" I find that amazing. Then again, it could be the new stock phrase of ghosts. Rather than telling people to get out, they are now telling everyone to get back to work. Sounds like a couple supervisors I've had over the years.

Investigating the Washoe Club

Reno Apparition Seekers Society (RASS) is made up of three men who enjoy ghost hunting: Jeff Frey, Jason Ball and Bruce Pollard. On a cold January night, they got together to do an overnight investigation of the Washoe Club. This would be the first investigation for newbie and somewhat skeptical Jason, who would work under the tutelage of seasoned investigators Jeff and Bruce. Their equipment consisted of the K-2 meter, digital cameras and recorders, dowsing rods, a full-spectrum camera and a green laser grid. And, like all good ghost investigators, they also had a few trigger objects. These were candy cigarettes, a deck of cards and recorded music from the 1860s.

First stop was the crypt. During an EVP session, Jeff asked if anyone had something to say to them, and someone certainly did.

"Get to work!" came the ghostly reply.

Jason was alone in the crypt when he heard a *ping* sound. "What was that?" he asked. Aiming his flashlight in the direction of the sound, he discovered an inch-long screw on the floor. *Could this have made the sound*, he wondered. He got his answer when he picked the screw up and dropped it to the ground. Yes, the same sound; he'd discovered the source of the *ping*. Someone had tossed the screw toward him but who? Maybe it was the ghostly kid Peter, who hangs out in an upstairs closet and throws things. Peter might have ventured down to the crypt to taunt the investigator. Later the men asked, "Who's here with us?" The response was, "Jerry."

They are currently doing research to determine if there was someone named Jerry connected to the Washoe Club. It's common to many haunted

RASS outside the Washoe Club. *Photo courtesy of Jeff Frey.*

Jason Ball using dowsing rods upstairs at the Washoe Club. *Photo courtesy Jeff Frey.*

locations for a ghost to announce itself by fragrance. During RASS's investigation, the overwhelming aroma of rose perfume followed them everywhere they went. Jeff believes it might have been the ghostly Lena, although she did not respond to EVP requests.

They got the most activity upstairs in the ballroom. Bruce began taking photos when his camera stopped working for no apparent reason. This is common to haunted locations. The belief is that ghosts zap the energy from electronic devices—either that or they deliberately cause them to malfunction. Assuming this might be the case, Jeff said, "Knock it off! Let him use his camera." And wouldn't you know it, the camera was working once more.

Later in the evening, Bruce started to dance and asked, "Do you want to dance with me?" The EVP response was, "Last chance."

When Jeff asked, "Is there anything you want us to do?" he received what he thought of as a humorous response: "Die."

This ghost had a sense of humor that was revealed later in the investigation. The men started to talk about Australia, Sasquatch and Mexico. "You go there," the voice said.

Jeff Frey walks off steps. Note the orbs visible upstairs at the Washoe Club. *Photo courtesy of Jeff Frey.*

Most ghost hunters will agree that a healthy amount of skepticism is a good thing. In this way, we are less likely to jump at shadows and more likely to obtain credible evidence. Because of all the activity, Jason was becoming less of a skeptic as the night wore on.

RASS's investigation lasted a total of eleven hours. The men returned to their rooms at the Silver Queen, exhausted but ready for the next investigation. And that is how ghost hunters are.

EPILOGUE

There is an old saying, "Where there is smoke, there is fire." I find this apropos whether I'm investigating ghosts or researching and collecting ghost stories. The fact that so many people who live and work in Virginia City have experienced ghosts served to convince me that this town is very haunted. It is why I believe VC to be one of the most haunted towns in the United States.

One person may visit a location and find it quite ordinary. Another may go to the same location and experience extraordinary phenomena. So it is with Virginia City. But make no mistake: Virginia City is much more than a small town perched atop a mountain. Virginia City is an experience unto itself. Visit once, and you'll fall under its spell. And you'll be back, again and again.

Writing about the ghosts and history of Virginia City, a special place to me, has been an enjoyable experience. I hope that you have found reading *Haunted Virginia City* an enjoyable experience as well.

In youth, when I did love, did love,
(To quote the Sexton's homely ditty)
I lived six thousand feet above
Sea level, in Virginia City.
The site was bleak, the houses small
The narrow streets unpaved and slanting,
But now it seems to me of all
The spots on earth the most enchanting.

Let art with all its cunning strive,
Let nature lavish all her splendor,
One touch of sentiment will give
A charm more beautiful and tender;
And so that town howe'er uncouth
To others who have chanced to go there
Enshrines the ashes of my youth,
And there is Fairyland—or nowhere.

Who tends its marts, who treads its ways
Are mysteries beyond my guessing,
To me the forms of other days
Are still about its centers pressing;
I know that loving lips are cold
And true hearts still—ah! more's the pity,
But in my fancy they yet hold
Their empire in Virginia City.

Unhallowed flames have swept away
The structures in which I delighted,
The streets are grass-grown and decay
Has left the sunny slopes benighted.
But not to me,—to my dim sight
The town is always like the olden,
As to the captive Israelite,
Shown aye Jerusalem the golden.

I would not care to see it now,
I choose to know it as I then did,
With glorious light upon its brow,
And all its features bright and splendid;
Nor would I like that it should see
Me, gray and stooped, a mark for pity,
And learn that time has dealt with me
As hard as with—Virginia City.

—"Virginia City," by Joseph Goodman,
publisher of Territorial Enterprise *and known as the man*
who hired Samuel Clemens to write for his newspaper, circa 1860

ABOUT THE AUTHOR

An independent historian, Janice volunteers at the Nevada Historical Society and is a past docent of the Fourth Ward School Museum in Virginia City. She is a member of the Western Writers of America and the author of numerous books on Nevada's history, true crime, unusual occurrences and hauntings. She speaks on these subjects throughout the state. Her Ghosthunting 101 and Nevada's Quirky Historical Facts classes for Community Education at Truckee Meadows Community College have been well received.